REMEMBERING SMITHFIELD

REMEMBERING SMITHFIELD
SKETCHES OF APPLE VALLEY

JIM IGNASHER

THE History PRESS

Published by The History Press
Charleston, SC 29403
www.historypress.net

Front cover image, top: Vintage postcard from Greenville, with the Waterman tavern in the background. *Author's collection. Front cover image, bottom*: Oscar Tobey's general store, with Harold Tobey Smith in front. *Courtesy of Ralph W. Batley. Back cover images, top to bottom*: Smith-Appleby House, *author's collection*; Helen Sumner Smith (left) and unknown girl, *courtesy of Priscilla W. Holt*; Henry Farnum Smith, with the Oscar Tobey House in the background, *courtesy of Priscilla W. Holt*.

Unless otherwise noted, all images are by the author.

First published 2009

Manufactured in the United States

ISBN 978.1.59629.679.4

Library of Congress Cataloging-in-Publication Data

Ignasher, Jim.
Remembering Smithfield : sketches of Apple Valley / Jim Ignasher.
p. cm.
Includes bibliographical references.
ISBN 978-1-59629-679-4
1. Smithfield (R.I. : Town)--History--Anecdotes. 2. Smithfield (R.I. : Town)--Social life and customs--Anecdotes. I. Title.
F89.S6I46 2009
974.5'1--dc22
2009015773

To Dorothy Swain, of the Greenville Public Library,
who suggested that I write this book,
and to Maggie Botelho, whose tireless efforts at the
Smith-Appleby House have not gone unnoticed.

Contents

Contents

INTRODUCTION

In 1881, Thomas Steere wrote a book called *History of the Town of Smithfield from its Organization, in 1730–1, to its Division, in 1871*. This rare book was the first publication pertaining to Smithfield. It was written in three chapters. Chapter 1 dealt with the life of Roger Williams and the establishment of Rhode Island. Chapter 2 began with the incorporation of Smithfield and went on to cite short excerpts from old town meeting records that dealt with important local issues between the years 1730 and 1871. Chapter 3 extensively covered the history of early manufacturing in Smithfield. The last portion of the book consisted of several appendices that listed the names of those who served in various town positions between 1730 and 1871. A lot has happened since Mr. Steere's book was published.

This book is not meant to be a duplication of Mr. Steere's work, but rather a continuation of it. It differs by covering topics that Mr. Steere did not, such as the Battle of Nipsachuck, the lost villages of Fountain Spring and Hanton City, the scandal that forced the closing of the town poor farm and how the railroads eventually came to Smithfield. This book also chronicles events that have occurred in Smithfield since Mr. Steere's work was published, such as the establishment of the fire and police departments, aviation history and the rise of the apple-growing industry.

It is the author's hope that in years hence, someone will continue to record the town's history for future generations, and perhaps write a book of their own.

Chapter 1

Before Smithfield Was Smithfield

Just where in the timeline does one start to write about the history of a town? Why, at the beginning of course, but which beginning? Should the story open when the town was formally established under state charter, or when it was first settled yet unincorporated? Does the history of a town start when the first Europeans arrived, or with the Native Americans who preceded them?

In starting this book, I asked myself these questions. As one who is interested in local history, I have hiked the woods of Smithfield and northern Rhode Island in search of abandoned colonial-era farm sites so that I may study and document them before they are lost to development. These sites can date anywhere from the mid-1600s to the late 1800s, and are readily identified by their stone walls and cellar holes. Anyone who has rambled through the woods of New England has no doubt come across such sites, and perhaps wondered about the people who once lived there.

However, in my travels, I have found other sites that are no doubt pre-colonial, i.e., Native American. These are perhaps hundreds, or even thousands, of years old. Some are definitely Native American, while others are carefully listed as "enigmatic" at this time, perhaps worthy of future study by those much more knowledgeable than I in these matters.

Prehistoric Smithfield

It is generally accepted that there are abandoned farm sites in the woods that are two or three centuries old, but many find it difficult to accept the idea that even older Native American sites exist in the same woods. Perhaps it is because Native American sites are not as obvious.

I have no background in archaeology or anthropology. Admittedly, my knowledge in such matters is limited to what I have read and studied on my own; however, when one considers the fact that native people lived in this area for literally thousands of years before the arrival of Europeans, one has to admit that there is a high probability that such sites exist. With that in mind, I decided to start this book with a brief—very brief—view of prehistoric Smithfield to give the reader a historical frame of reference.

Thirteen thousand years ago, during the last Ice Age, all of New England was covered by a massive glacier, which scientists believe was up to one mile thick in some places. The ice, weighing millions of tons, pushed forward like a giant bulldozer, grinding away hills and mountaintops and exposing the granite outcrops that are seen everywhere in northern Rhode Island today. Many of these granite outcrops still bear striations known as "glacial scarring" that indicate the direction in which the glacier traveled.

As global temperatures began to warm, the glacier began to melt, creating massive rushing rivers that further helped to shape the land. These rivers carried material made up of sand, soil, rocks and boulders. Granite rocks that had once been part of mountains were tumbled and tossed like pebbles in the tumultuous waters. This action wore their edges smooth and rounded

Stone walls such as this one were made by early European settlers using stones left behind by the melting glacier at the end of the last Ice Age.

This glacial erratic on Wolf Hill is approximately nine feet tall and thirteen feet wide. It was tumbled and carried to this spot during the last Ice Age. Boulders such as this can be found throughout the woods of Smithfield.

the rocks like the stones commonly found on a riverbed or a beach. As the water receded, these rocks were deposited literally everywhere across the landscape. It was these rocks left by the glacier that early European farmers used to construct the countless miles of stone walls that are seen today.

Avid hikers have no doubt noticed huge granite boulders randomly strewn about in local woods. Many are the size of an average automobile, and some even larger. Like the fieldstones, they were also left behind by the glacier and are known as "glacial erratics." Some of these erratics may have traveled many miles before they came to rest here in Smithfield.

In some cases, glacial erratics have been found perched on top of smaller stones. The arrangement of the stones leaves little doubt that they were positioned in this manner by the hand of man. Such formations are found throughout the American Northeast and Europe and are commonly referred to as "dolmen." The question is, who created such arrangements, and why? Some who have studied these sites believe them to be prehistoric. Researchers partly base their findings on the fact that there are no known records to indicate that such sites were created by early European settlers. Of the colonial-era diaries that have survived to the present day, none

This dolman is located on Wolf Hill. One can clearly see that it has been propped up by the hand of man. Many believe that such sites predate European settlement in America.

mentions the construction of perched boulder sites. It would also stand to reason that early European settlers had enough to keep themselves busy just trying to survive, and therefore wouldn't have had the time or the inclination to create such sites just to make modern researchers ask questions two hundred years later.

Smithfield has at least one dolmen, located on Wolf Hill. Two others are known to exist about two miles away in Johnston. Why they were constructed is open to interpretation, but the general belief is that they were ceremonial in nature. One seemingly common feature is that they are constructed on rocky outcroppings with a water source nearby.

There is much more that could be said on this subject, but that is not the focus of this book. In fact, several books have been written on the topic, as well as numerous articles published in the *NEARA Journal*, a publication of the New England Antiquities Research Association. The Wolf Hill site is mentioned here to illustrate that such sites exist in Smithfield regardless of who made them.

THE FIRST INHABITANTS OF SMITHFIELD

As the glacier receded and the Ice Age ended, the first people migrated to New England. They most likely followed game while looking for new territory to call their own. These Native Americans left no written history, but the stone tools and artifacts they left behind are still found in the area from time to time.

In the fourteenth and fifteenth centuries, Smithfield was the domain of the Nipmuc Indians, whose tribal territory extended into nearby Connecticut and Massachusetts. The name *Nipmuc* originates from the word *nipnet*, which is said to mean "small pond people" or "freshwater people."

The name Nipmuc has been spelled several different ways in old records, including Nipnet, Neepnet, Nipmug, Neepmuck, Neetmock and Neipnett.

The earliest European settlers of Smithfield no doubt had contact with the Nipmuc from time to time, and it appears that they coexisted peacefully up until King Philip's War in 1675.

THE BATTLE OF NIPSACHUCK

On August 1, 1675, an important battle in King Philip's War was fought in the area of Nipsachuck Swamp, which straddles the present-day Smithfield/North Smithfield town line. This incident later became known as the Battle of Nipsachuck.

Technically speaking, the battle took place in the town of Providence, because in 1675, Smithfield was considered part of the "outlands" of Providence. (Smithfield wasn't incorporated until 1730, fifty-five years after the battle, and North Smithfield wasn't incorporated until 1871.) In the 1600s, there were three major Native American tribes in Rhode Island. There were the Narragansett, spread across the southern area of the state; the Wampanoag, who occupied the northeastern portion of Rhode Island; and the Nipmuc, who lived in northwestern Rhode Island. Nipsachuck Swamp was in Nipmuc territory.

According to research done by Smithfield resident Michael Cavanagh, there are several different spellings for Nipsachuck, including Nipchossuck, Nipsachook, Nipsochoke and Nippsatchuck. The word means "water near the hill," which would describe Nipsachuck Swamp because the swamp lies at the base of Nipsachuck Hill.

King Philip's War lasted from June 1675 to October 1676. Philip, whose real name was Metacomet, was a Wampanoag. King Philip was the name given to him by the English.

The hostilities began on June 20, 1675, when a group of Native Americans conducted a raid on Swansea, Massachusetts, where several homes were burned and some settlers were killed. There are differing accounts as to what led to the raid, but the end result was that the citizens of Swansea were forced to flee the area for their own safety. Armed colonists from Bridgewater, Taunton and Boston were sent to help and the fighting continued for several days.

On June 30, colonial troops pursued Philip and his followers into the Mount Hope section of Bristol, but Philip managed to escape across the bay into Tiverton.

On July 19, another skirmish occurred, known as the Pocasset Swamp Fight, but again Philip escaped and fled north through Fall River. From there, he crossed the Taunton River and headed westward into northern Rhode Island, where on July 31, he and about two hundred others made camp near Nipsachuck Hill. When those looking for Philip learned of this, they made plans to attack the following morning. They took the camp by complete surprise and, during the fight, killed about thirty of Philip's men. Philip and the others retreated into Nipsachuck Swamp, where they waited out the rest of the day.

Here the battle stopped while the colonists waited for reinforcements. Fresh troops arrived about 10:00 a.m., but for reasons never explained, the commander failed to renew the attack for an additional twenty-four hours, thus allowing Philip and the others to escape. The colonials had superior numbers and weaponry, and historians believe that had they pressed forward they would have won the battle and ended the war then and there. Instead, what followed after Nipsachuck were further attacks by both sides throughout New England with the loss of many lives. The war finally ended on August 12, 1676, when Philip was killed at a skirmish in Bristol, Rhode Island.

Unfortunately, shortly before the war's end, there was a second skirmish at Nipsachuck. Depending on one's point of view, it was either a battle or a massacre. On July 1, 1676, local militia attacked a native campsite at Nipsachuck, routing the inhabitants into the swamp. Over the next three hours, 171 Native Americans were killed, 34 of them men. In addition, 41 women and children were taken prisoner.

Many of the battle sites connected with King Philip's War have historical markers, but one will not find any such markers at Nipsachuck Swamp, perhaps because the site itself is out of sight and, therefore, out of mind. What one will find along the western slope of Nipsachuck Hill leading down toward the swamp are piles of stones that serve no apparent purpose but are obviously man-made. Some think they may be Native American in origin, and are either the graves of those killed in the battle or are ceremonial in nature, marking the location of where the fight took place.

In 2007, these stone mounds were "discovered" when the area was slated for development. The widely publicized discovery led to a halt in the project, which has made its way into the court system. As of this writing, the future of this project is undecided.

Since the story of the mounds was reported in the press, other similar sites have been found in the areas surrounding Nipsachuck Hill. One site not far from where the battle took place reportedly has numerous stone mounds. Other sites have been discovered in Smithfield on Wionkhiege Hill and off Log Road.

There are those who say that the stone mounds are Native American in origin and that all of the sites subsequently discovered are related to Nipsachuck. On the other hand, there are those who claim that the rocks are simply random piles made by colonial-era farmers when they were clearing their land in preparation for farming.

Those serving in official archaeological capacities have termed the piles "enigmatic," citing no clear proof one way or the other. Excavations of such sites in the past have been inconclusive. It would seem that further study is needed.

THE LEGEND OF JOHN NOFORCE

In the woods just off Mann School Road is a high rock-faced cliff that was once known as Noforce Rocks but is all but ignored and forgotten today. The curious name is derived from the legend of a Native American named John Noforce, who is said to have fallen to his death from the top of the cliff. The tale comes down through local folklore, and like many legends, it has changed slightly with each retelling; but is it true? There is evidence to suggest that it is.

The legend was mentioned in a 1929 *Providence Journal* newspaper article, in which the story was related to the reporter by T.K. Winsor, who had heard it from his father, who in turn had heard it from his father.

Exactly how and when John met his end is unknown. One story goes that he jumped because of a Romeo and Juliet type of situation between his tribe and another. A follow-up story relates how the maiden whom John had been in love with threw herself from the same cliff upon learning of his death. Another version says that John jumped to escape an enemy who was pursuing him, choosing death before capture. Others have speculated that he simply slipped and fell by accident.

Did a Native American by the name of John Noforce really fall to his death from this fifty-foot cliff, or is it just a legend?

Possible proof that the legend is true appeared in the June 1969 edition of the *Hinterlander*, a publication of the Western Rhode Island Civic Historical Society. In an article submitted by Merrilla Steere, it was stated that in 1672, a man named John Steere bought a large tract of land on Wionkhiege Hill and subsequently deeded six acres to a man named Sam (not John) Noforce. The rocky ridge where the incident is said to have occurred was reportedly within these six acres. With this in mind, could the names of the two men have been intertwined, and Sam became John during the retelling of the story?

Further information comes from Lawrence J. Sasso Jr., editor of *Your Smithfield* magazine and owner of the land surrounding Noforce Rocks. Along the face of the rocky cliff is a cave of sorts carved out by the glacier in the last Ice Age, in which John Noforce is said to have lived. Items found by Mr. Sasso at the site would suggest that someone had once lived there.

There is no known grave for Mr. Noforce, nor is there any record of his death, but the legend lives on.

Chapter 2

Early Colonial Settlements

The first European settlers arrived in Smithfield in the late 1600s, at a time when the area was still part of the "outlands" of Providence. At that time, northern Rhode Island was still wilderness, with bears, wolves and other dangers lurking at every turn. Roads were nothing more than footpaths, and if one became hurt or lost, he was on his own. But the founding fathers knew that if the state was to grow and prosper, the "outlands" had to be settled. Therefore, large tracts of free land were offered by the Town of Providence to those brave enough to settle there.

Two of Smithfield's earliest settlements, Fountain Spring and Hanton City, are no longer in existence and are all but forgotten today.

The Vanished Village of Fountain Spring

The city of Pawtucket has the honor of being recognized as the "Birthplace of the American Industrial Revolution" because Samuel Slater built the first successful textile mill there in 1793. Unfortunately, history has overlooked a small manufacturing settlement that was once located between Greenville Avenue and Route 44 that predated Slater's mill by more than one hundred years. The settlement was known by different names, among them Reaper's Brook, Ripper's Brook, Skeeterville and Fountain Spring. What remained of the original colonial settlement was lost to development in the 1980s, but what makes this lost village historically significant is that besides being one of the earliest settlements in Smithfield, it was also the site of the second fulling mill in Rhode Island and what is believed to be the first mill in the country to manufacture machine parts for textile mills.

Although the name Fountain Spring appears on local maps as late as 1947, few Smithfield residents have ever heard of it, possibly because so little has been written about it. Research has uncovered three *Providence Journal* newspaper articles from 1905, 1918 and 1927. Some of the information contained in these articles is presented here.

The village was founded in 1663 by William Hawkins, who was granted fifty acres of land by the Providence Town Council with the stipulation that he had to live there for at least three years and obtain council approval before he could sell any portion of the land. Hawkins established his home along a stream known as Ripper's Brook, which is listed as Reaper's Brook on contemporary maps. Before long, others began to build nearby and the settlement grew.

In 1699, Hawkins partnered with Daniel Williams and built a fulling mill along Ripper's Brook, and Robert Sanders was hired to run it for them. Fulling mills operated by removing the dirt and oils from sheared sheep's wool and stretching it to reduce shrinkage so it could be spun into yarn. At that time, the only other fulling mill in Rhode Island was in Warwick. The Smithfield mill operated until about 1740, when it was converted to a sawmill.

In 1723, Sanders and Moses Bartlett built a second mill along the brook. The dam created to operate this mill formed Factory Pond.

In 1800, Nehemiah Hawkins converted the sawmill into a machine shop to produce loom parts for the booming cotton industry. He later built a three-story stone mill one hundred feet downstream. To power his new mill, Hawkins built a dam, which created present-day Hawkins Pond.

A Lost Cemetery

The village had a cemetery containing at least twenty-five graves; this cemetery has since disappeared, along with the rest of the settlement. Documentation that it once existed can be found in a *Providence Journal* article dated June 2, 1918, which stated that the cemetery was located on a prominence overlooking one of the two ponds. It was said that the names on most of the tombstones had been worn away over the years, but one stone with the name of Sanders could still be read.

In 1919, a man named James N. Arnold conducted a survey of every known cemetery in Smithfield, but for some reason this cemetery was never mentioned. However, Arnold did record a cemetery that today can easily be found on Factory Pond Drive (Smithfield Historical Cemetery #65), but this is clearly not the one mentioned in the *Providence Journal*.

What happened to the missing cemetery is anybody's guess. Perhaps it still exists somewhere in the remaining wooded area surrounding Reaper's Brook, but modern attempts to locate it have been unsuccessful.

The Nineteenth Century

It appears that the original name of the settlement was Ripper's Brook, which later morphed into Reaper's Brook. About 1830, the name Skeeterville appeared, which seems to indicate that mosquitoes infested the area. The name was later changed to Fountain Spring in the 1850s.

In 1831, Daniel Harkness and Isaac Saunders were producing cotton cloth at one of the mills. An 1851 map of Smithfield produced by H.F. Walling indicates a mill at the village known as the "Fisk and Aldrich Mill." A Beers Atlas map of 1870 indicates that one mill was still in production as a "shoddy" or woolen mill. It was at some point after 1870 that the area fell into decline for reasons that are unclear. Perhaps it was because of the proliferation of more modern woolen mills in Greenville and Johnston.

In 1892, the mill and surrounding property was purchased by Greenville businessman Nicholas Winsor, who sold it in 1904 to a Providence dentist named Frederick W. Thrift, who wanted to convert the property to a summer recreational area. He lived on the property until 1920, but his venture failed. In 1921, Doctor A.W. Hughes of Esmond bought the land and had the old mill and other buildings demolished for safety reasons.

There is a road leading off Greenville Avenue known today as Hughes Drive, apparently named for Dr. Hughes. The road appears on maps dating to the 1800s, and some of the houses that line it would indicate that it dates to the latter days of the settlement. This is about all that remains of what was once Fountain Spring.

In the late twentieth century, housing subdivisions were built on land where the old village once stood. Street names such as Factory Pond Drive, Reaper Court and Fountain Spring Lane reflect the area's past.

HANTON CITY, SMITHFIELD'S LOST CITY

Buried in the woods in the northern part of Smithfield lay the remains of a colonial-era ghost town known as Hanton City. The area has been the subject of speculation and folklore for generations. Questions such as who lived there; when did they live there; and, most importantly, what happened to them have been asked over the years, with various replies.

The main reason for all of the questions is the lack of information on the subject. Hanton City isn't indicated on old maps of Smithfield or mentioned in old town records. Nor is it mentioned in Thomas Steere's 1881 book about the history of Smithfield. This lack of information has only added to the mystery. The cellar holes, a graveyard and stone walls are proof that a settlement once existed, but why no official mention of it?

Longtime residents tell of several legends as to the origins and inhabitants of Hanton City. One story goes that the settlement was made up of ex-slaves and Native Americans who were forced to live in seclusion because they were not welcome elsewhere in the town. Another states that people from the town's poor farm were sent to live there. A third story goes that British soldiers who deserted during the American Revolution settled the area. An offshoot to this story tells of a British soldier who deserted during the Revolution and married into the Hanton family. Still another story claims that ex-prison inmates established the settlement. Any of these stories may explain why the settlement was never mentioned in books or indicated on maps, but are they true?

There are several theories as to what happened to the population of Hanton City. A popular one is that they were wiped out by a plague. Another says that they had their land confiscated for refusing to serve in the American Revolution because they were loyal to the king of England. A contradiction to that story is that they all left to fight in the Revolution and never returned. Still others think a natural disaster ended the settlement. A less romantic theory states that the land was settled by people who failed at farming and simply moved on.

This stone-lined cellar hole is all that is left of a house that once stood on this spot more than two hundred years ago. Cellar holes such as this are found throughout Hanton City.

Thus, Hanton City is steeped in mystery and folklore. Sometimes folk stories contain at least a grain of truth from which they originate.

How Hanton City Got Its Name

How did Hanton City get its name? The commonly accepted answer is that it was named for the Hanton family who once lived there. However, it seems that Hanton wasn't their real name. Their real name appears to have been Harrendeen, Herenden, Herndon or one of fourteen other ways of spelling it, as found in old town records. In fact, all seventeen variations are actually corruptions of the name Harrington. Therefore, Harrington became Harrendeen, which became Hanton and, hence, Hanton City.

Why was it called a city? That is open to interpretation. The Hantons were a large family, and other families also lived in the area, but the remains of the settlement are nowhere near big enough to even be called a town, let alone a city. However, there are indications that suggest that Hanton City may have been larger and spread out farther to the north into the present-day town of North Smithfield, which was part of Smithfield until 1871. Looking at contemporary maps of North Smithfield, one will see that there is a Hanton Road on the north side of Route 146 near the Woonsocket line.

A book titled *The History of North Smithfield*, by Walter A. Nebiker, published in 1976 by New England History Press, has a map that indicates that a tract of land was owned by a Benjamin Herendeen in what is today North Smithfield.

Other Names for Hanton City

Hanton City has also been called Island Woods or Islands in the Woods due to its topography of high, rocky, wooded hills rising out of the many swamps and wetlands in the area.

In the early 1800s, it was also called the Rumbly, presumably because of the rough roads and rough country that travelers passed through on their way from Stillwater to Woonsocket. Hanton City was also referred to as Cedar Swamp, as there is a large cedar swamp right in the middle of it.

As far back as the 1880s, Hanton City has also been referred to as Haunted City. There are two explanations for this. The generally accepted one is that "Haunted City" is simply a corruption of the name Hanton City that came about when the place became deserted.

The second explanation would imply that only ghosts inhabit the place now, or that the area is a ghost town. Historical research has not uncovered any stories of horrific events having taken place there that could be a basis for

Some of the inhabitants of Hanton City had talent when it came to working with stone, as evidenced by the stone shelf set into the wall of this cellar hole.

a ghost story, but local author Thomas D'Agostino recounts some anecdotal stories in his book *Haunted Rhode Island*, published by Schiffer Press in 2006.

Researching Hanton City

The cellar holes and stone walls in Hanton City have been curiosities for many years. Early attempts at researching Hanton City probably began sometime in the late 1800s, after the village had been abandoned and people with firsthand knowledge began to disappear.

Perhaps the earliest investigation into what happened to the residents of Hanton City took place in 1889, when a *Providence Journal* reporter ventured into the area and interviewed Thomas Hanton, age eighty, and his sister, who were living in a small shanty on the outskirts of Hanton City and were said to be the "last of the Hantons." The story was published in the *Providence Journal* on October 6, 1889, entitled, "A Buried City." This article is the earliest known documentation of Hanton City and focused on the history of the settlement as related by Tom Hanton.

The article indicated that Hanton City had been in its prime in the 1730s, which would mean it was already in existence when Smithfield was first incorporated. It also stated that newcomers to Smithfield referred to the area as "Haunted City," which indicates that the term was in use during the nineteenth century, yet the writer points out that longtime residents viewed the term with "amused contempt."

Tom Hanton was born in the area about 1809. The residents of Hanton City were poor, and Hanton related how when a justice of the peace married a couple in the area, he would be paid with a good meal and a jug of rum.

The people of Hanton City were primarily tanners and boot makers who sold their handmade goods at markets in Providence, but the advent of mills that could produce the same products faster and cheaper affected the settlement economically.

When asked about what happened to the people of Hanton City, Mr. Hanton explained simply, "They had all got poor, and sold out to anybody, and died off." His statement indicates that the populace of Hanton City wasn't wiped out by a plague or natural disaster, nor did they have their land confiscated.

Even though the article answered some questions pertaining to Hanton City, others still remained. It doesn't take long for information to become lost, and nearly fifty years after the 1889 *Providence Journal* article appeared, the historical information it contained was all but forgotten. By the early twentieth century, what happened to the people of Hanton City was once again a mystery.

One local resident who researched Hanton City was Agnes R. Maroney of Stillwater. In 1936, she presented a two-page paper on Hanton City to the Smithfield Historical Society based on her interview with Edwin C. Harris, age ninety, one of the oldest residents of Smithfield at the time.

One story that Mr. Harris had heard as a boy concerned a British soldier who deserted and married a girl from Hanton City. Another recalled a small stone shed with a jug of rum and a loaf of gingerbread placed in front of it where passing travelers could rest and refresh themselves. It was hoped that they would leave a coin or two before moving on. Mr. Harris added that many of the inhabitants were said to be tanners and boot makers.

Among Mr. Harris's recollections was a limerick that hinted of an interracial relationship:

Up in Hanton City,
There lived a very tall man.
He had a handsome daughter,
And her name was Hittiean.
She was courted by Lords & Dukes,
And by many a wealthy Knight,

But no one but Philip the Darkey
Could gain her heart's delight.

A final piece of information contained in Miss Maroney's paper concerns the variations of the name Harrington, Herrindeen and Hanton. It appears that even members of the same family couldn't decide on the proper spelling of their name.

Miss Maroney related a story in which three brothers were summoned to court in Woonsocket. As they were sworn in to give testimony, they each gave different names. One identified himself as Wanton Harrindeen, a second as Welcome Harrington and a third as Tom Hanton. When the judge demanded an explanation, the three just told him that was how they say it.

This last piece of information from the paper appears under Miss Maroney's name and looks as if it may have been added as an afterthought. The words "probably" and "probable" accompanying the quoted words of the Hantons would seem to indicate that the story was anecdotal and not actually taken from a printed court record.

Mr. Harris was interviewed again in 1937 by Franklin N. Strickland, a reporter for the *Providence Journal*, and was featured in an article that appeared in that paper on February 14, 1937. The article primarily focused on finding a Hanton City landmark known as "the Threshing Rock," a large granite outcrop formed when the glacier receded thousands of years ago. Legend has it that both Native Americans and early settlers used it to thresh their grain in a naturally formed hollow in the rock. In the late 1800s and early 1900s, before the woods had reclaimed the area, the rock commanded a view of Cedar Swamp and was said to be a popular picnic destination.

Two other Hanton City researchers were Joe L. St. Pierre and Martha O. Tanner, a writer for *The Observer*, which today is known as *The Valley Breeze & Observer*. Together they explored Hanton City and the Threshing Rock. Mrs. Tanner wrote about their excursion in an article that appeared in *The Observer* on May 25, 1972.

One of the photographs that accompanied Mrs. Tanner's article showed four standing stone pillars that are located near the remains of a cellar hole. The caption likened them to a "miniature Stonehenge" and questioned what they were. The answer came the following week when Mrs. Beverly Dobson of the Smithfield Historic Preservation Commission wrote *The Observer* and identified the pillars as the remains of a corncrib.

After reading Martha Tanner's article, Margery I. Mathews of Foster wrote a letter to *The Observer* that included information as to the origin of Hanton City. Her letter appeared on June 15, 1972, as follows:

According to legend, the natural depression in the Threshing Rock was used by both early settlers and Native Americans to thresh grain. The rock can be found at coordinates 41.94388 N, 71.52226 W. *Courtesy of Andrew C. Allin.*

One Hanton City farm site has a large stone wall that fords a stream. The rocks in the wall are big and no doubt took a great deal of labor to move into place.

These standing stones mentioned in Martha Tanner's 1972 *Observer* article are said to be the remains of an old corncrib.

These standing stones at one of the former home sites are often confused as graves, but they are not. Although some think that they may predate the settlement of Hanton City, they are most likely the remains of another corncrib.

Editor;

One clue to the settlers of Hanton City, the subject of Martha Tanner's entertaining story, may be found in the oral traditions of the Foster branch of the Harrington family.

"I've always known that Harringtons lived up there," says my father, Herman Harrington repeating what he had learned from his father, Wheaton, who, describing early variant spellings of the name (Hearnton, Hearnden, Herendeen, to name a few), said that Hanton Road in Smithfield was a derivation.

Following this clue and looking under Hearnton in the early Providence Records and Deed Books, one finds that Benjamin Hearnton Sr., who settled in Providence between 1647-1651, acquired through various transactions, some of the Common land 10 miles north of Providence. It was bounded by the "highway that separated it from Edward Inman's Wasquadomsett section between the Pawtucket (Blackstone) and Wasquadomsett (Crookfall) rivers." Lands Belonging to Daniel Brown, (a son in law of Benjamin's), Lawrence Wilkinson and James Balloo were mentioned as bounds. It is land described as "part upland, part swamp."

Benjamin Sr. deeded parcels to four of his sons; Benjamin Jr., Joseph, William, and Issac. Ruth Eddy, in a family history, (a copy is available at the R.I. Historical Society) places the settlement "somewhat east of the present village of Primrose." Information from several old maps tends to confirm the Hanton City Road area as the general location. References in later records and deeds show that the four brothers with their large families did settle there.

In May, 1883, Ben Jr., and Joseph entered a complaint to the magistrate that "the highway up into the country was stopped by Elmer Whipple." Action was convened until the June meeting when five men were appointed to open the highway to the Cedar Swamp. Swampy land is mentioned in the deeds and shown on some maps so the reference probably is the same Cedar Swamp that Mrs. Tanner valiantly explored.

Identifying the first settlers of Hanton City doesn't detract from the mystery but, perhaps, sets the scene for the next installment! Benjamin Junior's wife and daughter were both named Lidia: was the Lydia Ann Trail named for one?

Margery I. Mathews,
Foster

The "next installment" Ms. Mathews spoke of came rather quickly. Other people contacted Mrs. Tanner with what they knew about Hanton City, and she and Mr. St. Pierre set out to verify the information.

In researching Smithfield Record Book #1, they found information that indicated that Hanton City was settled by three related families with the surnames of Paine, Henended and Shepey, aka Paine, Hanton and Shippee. They were English, as were many early settlers to Smithfield, of a social class known as yeomen or freemen, which put them near the bottom of the social ladder of the day.

Further research revealed that family names of Hanton City residents could also be found in records listing those who served in King Philip's War in 1675–76. After the war, some were given land as payment for their service. Although there were no specific records indicating that land in Hanton City was granted in this way, it was surmised that the Hantons and others could have been granted the land at that time. Even though it was poor land, it was still land, and at that time, land ownership gave one higher social status and the right to vote.

Their research also revealed that a Herendon was always serving in some capacity in town affairs up until the time of the American Revolution. In

Some of the stone walls that crisscross the landscape of Hanton City are nearly three centuries old. They denote the boundaries of old fields where animals grazed and crops were grown.

These stones are all that remain of a structure that was built against this hillside. What the building was used for is unknown. The home sites were generally located on higher ground.

checking a roster of the Continental militia for 1775 through 1779, Mrs. Tanner didn't find any names associated with Hanton City, but some Hanton City names were still found in town records in the 1790s after the Revolution.

Joe St. Pierre followed up on an article written by Florence P. Simister that appeared in the 1972 *Rhode Island Yearbook* entitled "Rhode Island Exodus," which indicated that some men from Smithfield bought land in St. Johnsbury, Vermont, for one dollar per acre after the Revolution. St. Pierre traveled to St. Johnsbury and discovered former Hanton City names in town records, indicating that at least some residents of Hanton City left after the Revolution.

To document what they had found, Mrs. Tanner wrote another article entitled "Hanton City Revisited," which appeared in *The Observer* on August 10, 1972.

Hanton City, Fact versus Folklore

After considering all the available information, it seems many of the questions about Hanton City can now be answered.

The area was not settled by freed slaves or Native Americans. This story may have its origins in the limerick mentioned by Agnes Maroney about

Hittiean and Philip the Darkey. If the limerick is taken literally, then we are to assume that it is based on two actual people. Hittiean may be a corruption of the name Lydia Ann, and there was a Lydia Ann Road in Hanton City that ran from Douglas Pike to where North Central Airport is today. It's not known who Philip the Darkey really was, but it can be surmised that he was dark in complexion. Although it is possible that former slaves may have stayed in the area during the Civil War when the Underground Railroad was in operation, historical evidence shows that they were not the first settlers to the area.

Native Americans did of course inhabit the area before the arrival of Europeans; however, they did not construct the cellar holes and stone walls that define the area today.

Ex-inmates from the town's poor farm did not settle Hanton City either. The Town of Smithfield operated a poor farm and asylum on Douglas Pike from 1835 to 1871.The poor farm was established well after the founding of Hanton City, and upon its closing, all inmates were transferred elsewhere. (For more information about the poor farm, see Chapter 5.)

The legend of AWOL British soldiers founding Hanton City may have arisen from a passage in Agnes Maroney's paper telling of a "deserter from

There is one known cemetery in Hanton City. Two stones have crude initials and dates carved in them. Research indicates that they are the graves of Alice Herendeen and her husband, Daniel Brown.

Besides being boot makers and tanners, the men of Hanton City also quarried huge blocks of granite for use in building foundations in Providence. These stones were cut by hand using the "pin and feather" method.

the British Army" marrying into one of these families. The American Revolution was fought between 1775 and 1783, one hundred years or so after the first settlers came to the Hanton City area. The Hantons, the Shippees and the Paines were in fact English, and according to previous researchers, records indicate that they fought in King Philip's War. Therefore, they were soldiers, but not deserters.

There is no evidence to suggest that a population of ex-prison inmates settled in the area. This story most likely originates as an off-shoot of the freed slaves/poor farm refugees/inmates theory.

Research conducted by Martha Tanner and Joe St. Pierre indicates that the area was first settled by three English families who were possibly granted the land as payment for service in King Philip's War. This would mean they arrived shortly after 1676.

When Was Hanton City Abandoned?

This question requires some speculation. The February 14, 1937 *Providence Journal* article mentions a cellar hole with a large ash tree estimated to be about one hundred years old growing out of it. When one takes into account that the tree could not have begun to grow until after the house had rotted away from neglect, it puts the time that the settlement was abandoned around the early 1800s, probably between 1800 and 1815.

Of course, there are some variables at play here. Was the tree one hundred years old, or older or younger? Assuming for the sake of argument that the tree was one hundred years old, one could surmise that abandonment of the settlement was begun by the 1820s. Then this raises the question of what happened to cause everyone to leave the area.

Historical research seems to negate the theories of a plague, natural calamity or land confiscation as the reasons for the demise of Hanton City. Furthermore, Tom Hanton makes no mention of these in the October 1889 *Providence Journal* article. Instead, he cites economic hard times.

There is also the Industrial Revolution to consider. In the late 1700s and early 1800s, mills were being built all along the Blackstone and Woonasquatucket Rivers. Besides being able to produce goods faster and cheaper than those made by hand, they also offered younger people an opportunity to earn steady wages and allow hope for a better way of life. The mills tended to be located in larger settlements or cities, which offered more services and distractions than rural country living. When faced with the prospect of backbreaking quarry work, tanning hides or farming, it is understandable that the younger people of Hanton City opted to leave to work in the mills, much like younger people today are being drawn away from the family farms in the Midwest for better-paying jobs in cities. Therefore, it is entirely possible that Hanton City was almost completely abandoned by the 1830s or 1840s.

As to the question of why Hanton City is not indicated on old maps, the answer seems to be that by the time the first maps of Smithfield were produced by H.F. Walling in the 1850s, the settlement was for all intents already abandoned. It had no manufacturing base like other areas of the town, and nothing of any historical significance took place there. Thomas Steere most likely didn't mention Hanton City in his book for the same reasons. It is interesting to note, however, that Steere did mention many of the names of persons associated with Hanton City, so it is not as if the area was purposefully ignored.

The only remaining mystery to Hanton City seems to be this: if several large families lived in Hanton City for a period of more than 120 years, then where are the people buried? As of this writing, only one small cemetery has been located in Hanton City. Where are the others?

Chapter 3
The Incorporation and Division of Smithfield

By 1730, the population of the "outlands" of Providence had reached the point where there was talk of municipal incorporation, meaning that the land would be set apart into one or more townships, one of which would be called Smithfield. There were several advantages to Smithfield's incorporation. Not having to go to Newport or Providence to pay taxes and settle local disputes was a main reason, as travel in those days left much to be desired. Incorporation would also allow for self-government rather than forcing residents to be subject to the will of those who seldom, if ever, visited the "outlands."

At the time of Smithfield's incorporation, the population of the town was between 400 and 450 people, with a majority being farmers who possessed a spirit of self-reliance and independence.

Naming Smithfield

There are two theories as to how the name of Smithfield was chosen for the new town.

One theory states that the name was adopted due to the large number of families by the name of Smith living in the area. However, this would have been true in many areas as Smith was, and still is, a common name.

The other theory states that the town was named for Smithfield, England, where some of the early settlers are said to have emigrated from. However, Smithfield, England, was not a town, but a marketplace that began as livestock fields just outside of the city of London during the Middle Ages. The area outside of London was originally known as "Smooth Field," which later morphed into "Smithfield." From 1133 to 1855, the site was used for a number of activities, including fairs, sporting competitions, a farmers' market and public executions. After 1855, it became known as Smithfield Market, and it is still thriving today.

So which of the two theories is correct? That remains open to speculation, as there do not appear to be any official records pertaining to the naming of the town. Perhaps there were some families named Smith who came to New England from this area of London.

The Early Days of Incorporation

The Town of Smithfield was incorporated at a meeting of the General Assembly held in Newport in February 1730. Newport was the capital of Rhode Island at that time. The towns of Glocester and Scituate were also established at the same meeting, thereby dividing the "outlands" into three separate towns. Foster was later set apart from Scituate in 1781, and Burrillville from Glocester in 1806.

In 1730, Central Falls was part of Smithfield. Central Falls began as a small village, but due to its proximity to Providence and Pawtucket, it grew rather quickly. At the time of Smithfield's incorporation, Central Falls was more developed than most of the town and unofficially became Smithfield Proper, where town business and meetings were conducted. This is why the oldest Smithfield town records, those dating from 1730 to 1870, are kept at the Central Falls City Hall. The present-day Smithfield Town Hall only has town records dating back to the town division in 1871. If one seeks any records older than 1730, they must go to the Providence City Hall.

As a side note, Central Falls was originally known as Chocolateville or Chocolate Mills due to a chocolate factory that was once located there. It wasn't until 1824 that the name was changed to Central Falls at the suggestion of Stephen Jenks, a locally prominent businessman of the day. It is said that the name was chosen because Central Falls is located between Valley Falls in Cumberland and the waterfalls at Slater Mill in Pawtucket.

The first Smithfield town meeting was held at the home of Captain Valentine Whitman on March 17, 1730. At the meeting, John Arnold, Joseph Mowry, Thomas Steere, Samuel Aldrich, John Mowry and Benjamin Smith were chosen as Smithfield's first town council. Other town officers were also chosen.

A NEW TOWN EMERGES

At the next town meeting, held on March 23, 1730, representatives for the Rhode Island General Assembly were chosen, as well as a quota of jurors for the courts in Providence. It was also decided that due to the proliferation of wildcats and wolves, the town would pay a bounty for killing them. It can be surmised that Wolf Hill gets its name from the packs of wolves that once roamed there.

In 1738, sixteen highway districts were established for the purpose of maintaining better roads. All able-bodied men over the age of twenty-one were required to work at least six days a year on maintaining the roads within the district in which they lived. Town-appointed inspectors made sure the work was carried out properly. Apprentices, slaves and "idiots" were exempted from this requirement.

During the American Revolution, Smithfield established three companies of troops, each composed of thirty men, with each company commanded by a captain. To entice enlistments, a sign-on bonus was offered: forty-eight shillings for recruits who had their own weapons and equipment and thirty-six shillings for those who did not.

In 1775, a committee was formed to collect one hundred firearms and get them in good working order at town expense. The weapons were to be hidden in three strategic locations within the town in the event of a British invasion. This strategy was employed in many towns during the war in case individual arms were confiscated.

In 1776, the Smithfield and Cumberland Rangers were established as a regiment separate and apart from the three foot companies already in Smithfield. In January 1777, at their own request, the rangers were sent to active duty.

Throughout the rest of the war, Smithfield, like all other communities, was required to supply certain quotas of goods and services to the government for the war effort. The quotas included everything from food and clothing to men, money and weapons.

Almost ninety years before the Civil War, residents of Smithfield made it known that they were against the buying and selling of slaves. In June 1783, a letter was sent to the Rhode Island General Assembly asking for a law prohibiting ship captains using Rhode Island ports from engaging in the slave trade.

In 1791, a local militia group consisting of fifty-three men known as the Smithfield Grenadiers was established, commanded by Captain Samuel McClellan. The following year, another independent company known as the Federal Protectors was formed under the command of Captain Zenas Winsor.

Smithfield's first library was the Wionkhiege Library, which was established in 1796 as a subscription library, which meant that members paid to belong. The collection was kept in the home of Job Mowry, the town's first librarian.

In 1797, the Rhode Island General Assembly allowed for the incorporation of the Smithfield Third Library. Why it was named the "Third Library" is unknown. Other early libraries included the one established by the Baptist church in Greenville in 1821 and the library established by the Georgiaville Cotton Manufacturing Company in 1827.

In 1805, the Smithfield Turnpike Authority was incorporated for the purpose of planning and constructing a direct route from Providence to Douglas, Massachusetts. The result was the road we know today as Douglas Pike or Route 7.

The word "pike" is short for turnpike, which was a toll road with gates set at certain intervals where travelers are required to stop and pay a toll. The money collected was supposed to go toward maintaining the road. Some frequent travelers managed to find "shortcuts" around the tollgates, thus shunning the toll. These shortcuts became known as "shun pikes," a street name that is still found in some city and town directories today.

It was also in 1805 that the Smithfield Union Bank was established in what is today Slatersville. Other early banks included the New England Pacific Bank, established 1818; the Smithfield Exchange Bank, established 1822; Smithfield Lime Rock Bank, established 1828; and the Providence County Bank, established 1834.

In early America, public lotteries were a popular way to raise funds for certain municipal building projects such as schools, bridges, churches and roads. All lotteries had to be sanctioned by the state to be considered legal. In October 1807, a lottery was held for the construction of the Smithfield Meeting House. The term "meetinghouse" had different meanings in the nineteenth century. Churches were known as meetinghouses, but a meetinghouse could also be where town meetings were held. The location of the Smithfield Meeting House has been lost to history, as the building no longer exists, but it is interesting to note that some of the tickets from this lottery have survived and are currently in the possession of the Historical Society of Smithfield.

In August 1821, it was voted to build a "Town House" in a centralized part of town so citizens in outlying areas would not have to trek to Central Falls to attend town meetings. The town house stood just north of Lydia Ann Road on Douglas Pike. (This portion of Lydia Ann Road ceased to exist

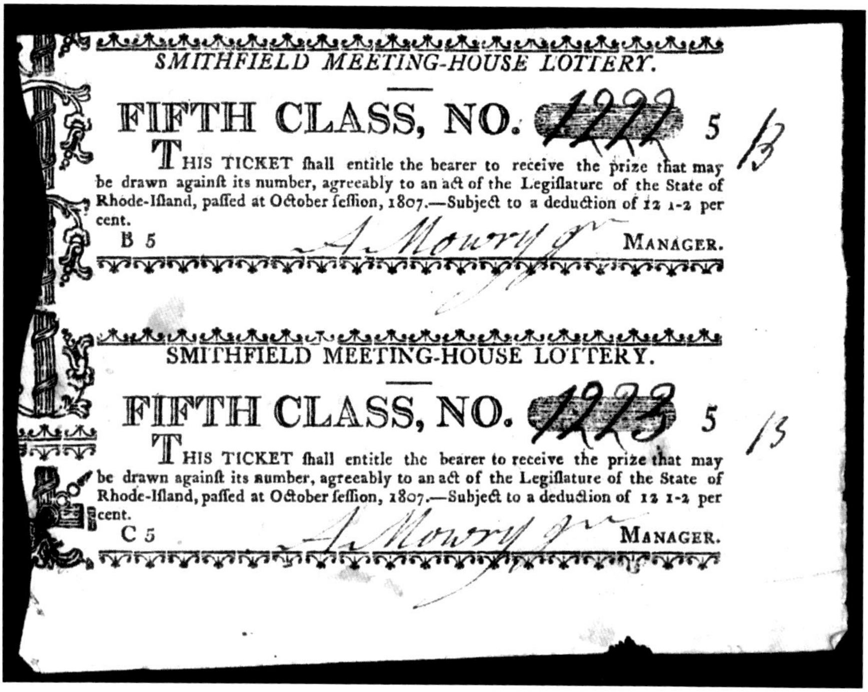

SMITHFIELD MEETING-HOUSE LOTTERY.

FIFTH CLASS, NO. 5

THIS TICKET ſhall entitle the bearer to receive the prize that may be drawn againſt its number, agreeably to an act of the Legiſlature of the State of Rhode-Iſland, paſſed at October ſeſſion, 1807.—Subject to a deduction of 12 1-2 per cent.

B 5 MANAGER.

SMITHFIELD MEETING-HOUSE LOTTERY.

FIFTH CLASS, NO. 5

THIS TICKET ſhall entitle the bearer to receive the prize that may be drawn againſt its number, agreeably to an act of the Legiſlature of the State of Rhode-Iſland, paſſed at October ſeſſion, 1807.—Subject to a deduction of 12 1-2 per cent.

C 5 MANAGER.

In 1807, a lottery was held to raise funds to build a meetinghouse in Smithfield. The building is long gone, but some of the lottery tickets have survived.

as of November 2008.) The building fell into disuse after the division of the town in 1871.

Smithfield began as an agricultural community, but as time went on, mill construction brought industry to the area. The mills brought jobs and an alternative to farm life, and villages grew up around them. The villages brought commerce, and commerce brought the railroads. By 1870, the population of Smithfield had reached 16,537 people. Smithfield had become a prosperous and affluent town, but there were those who wanted to change things.

THE DIVISION OF THE TOWN

About 1870, an idea was proposed that the town of Smithfield be divided into three separate towns. Not everyone was in favor of the notion, and both sides emphatically stated their opinions. As a point of fact, the idea was not a new one, as proposals for dividing the town had been submitted as early as 1838 and again in 1843. But it wasn't until 1870 that the idea really took hold.

Why would someone propose to divide the town in the first place? The answer is long and complicated, yet so simple—power. Dividing the town would add two additional members to the Rhode Island Senate, create two additional town councils and create other town officers in the new communities. Dividing the town meant some would gain political power while others would lose it. Therefore, the debate raged on.

Opponents to the division claimed that the towns would end up being governed by wealthy corporations, i.e., mill owners. Mill owners were influential people of the day who naturally wanted what would be best for their businesses, but some feared that their influence over local issues would grow if the town was divided.

One stipulation that most pro-division advocates agreed upon was that the town had to be divided in such a way that each new town would have the same approximate wealth and industry. The bone of contention among those in favor of the division was exactly where the new boundary lines should be drawn.

A partial attempt at division occurred in the late 1860s when it was suggested that a northeast portion of Smithfield be annexed to Woonsocket. This included the villages of Bernon, Globe, Hamlet and part of Waterford. These were areas that included factories and mills south of the Blackstone River. Of course, the citizens of Woonsocket were in favor of acquiring these industrial centers, but many in Smithfield were opposed. The matter came to a vote at a town meeting held in 1870. The results were 42 in favor, 193 opposed.

Even though the annexation to Woonsocket had failed, those in favor of dividing the town were undaunted and renewed their efforts at division. The movement apparently gained momentum because on January 21, 1871, a special town meeting was called to take another vote on the matter. This time the vote was to decide whether to divide Smithfield into three separate towns, as well as to annex the northeast portion to Woonsocket.

At the meeting, Thomas Steere spoke in front of a map that had lines drawn where the present-day boundaries of the towns of Smithfield, Lincoln and North Smithfield are located. The lines showed the old town of Smithfield divided into three almost equal parts. The northern portion, present-day North Smithfield, showed an area of about twenty-seven square miles, with seventy-five miles of highways, and a property valuation of $3,500,000. The southern portion, present-day Smithfield, would cover about twenty-six square miles, with about the same amount of highways and

$1,750,000 in taxable property. The southeast portion, present-day Lincoln and Central Falls, would be the smallest area and would only have about forty miles of highways, but to make up for that, it would have $5,000,000 in taxable property.

Apparently, Steere spoke eloquently and convincingly, for 111 voted in favor and 33 voted against. The measure was passed.

The next question became what to call the newly formed towns. That debate almost required a score card to keep up. In 1871, Central Falls was considered the industrial center of Smithfield and was referred to as "Smithfield Proper." Therefore, the area comprising present-day Lincoln and Central Falls was originally going to retain the name of Smithfield. Present-day Smithfield, being located to the west, was to be called West Smithfield, while the northern portion would be called North Smithfield. However, things didn't work out that way.

When North Smithfield was incorporated, the town was originally named Slater, in honor of mill owner John Slater, but sixteen days later, the name was changed to North Smithfield.

The town that was to be called Smithfield was incorporated as Lincoln in honor of Abraham Lincoln. Central Falls at that time was only a village in the town of Lincoln. It wasn't until 1895 that Central Falls incorporated and became the state's smallest city.

Of interest is the fact that not everyone was in favor of adopting the name of Lincoln for the new town, since it was supposed to have been called Smithfield. Some felt that they had been robbed of their right to be called Smithfield, and alleged eleventh-hour "shady dealings" by members of the General Assembly, who at the last minute changed the name when the town charter was granted. It was reported in the *Woonsocket Patriot* on March 31, 1871, "The inhabitants of this town will not yield without a struggle what they consider just and proper rights." Despite any protests, the name of Lincoln stuck.

Since Lincoln was not calling itself Smithfield, there was no reason for the western portion of the division to call itself West Smithfield. Therefore, the residents opted to retain the name as we know it today—Smithfield.

The first official meeting of the new town of Smithfield was held on June 10, 1871. At the meeting, the new town council was sworn in and William P. Steere was chosen council president. Other town officials were also sworn in. Afterward, a committee was appointed to deal with any unfinished business pertaining to "old" Smithfield.

After the division of the town, the new town of Smithfield contained a population of 2,605 people.

Smithfield Town Seals

One may be surprised to learn that Smithfield did not adopt a town seal until the early 1900s, nearly two hundred years after its incorporation. Before that time, a town council seal was utilized when necessary. The town council seal was a plain round stamp that read simply, "Town Council, Smithfield, R.I."

Smithfield's first official town seal was adopted sometime between 1913 and 1928. This information is based on a book by Howard M. Chapin, published in 1913, entitled, *Illustrations of the Seals, Arms, And Flags of Rhode Island.* In his book, Chapin noted that the towns of Smithfield and Barrington had no town seals. However, on September 16, 1928, the *Providence Journal* published an article written by Chapin that showed the seals used by all of Rhode Island's municipalities, and Smithfield's seal was among them. Unfortunately, going page by page through the Smithfield Town Council record books from 1913 to 1928 failed to find any notations proclaiming the adoption of a town seal. This is surprising considering what other town business was recorded.

Smithfield's first town seal depicted a shield with three hammers divided by a chevron. (In some representations there were three chevrons.) The placement of the hammers in conjunction with the chevron is reminiscent of an Old English coat of arms. In fact, there are literally thousands of examples of English coats of arms that are laid out in this manner, with the

The Smithfield Town Council Seal has been in use since 1871 and is still used today.

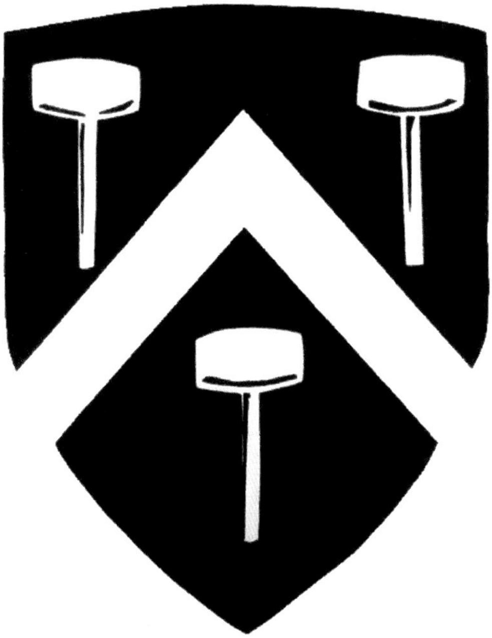

Smithfield's first town seal.

Smithfield's second town seal was only used briefly.

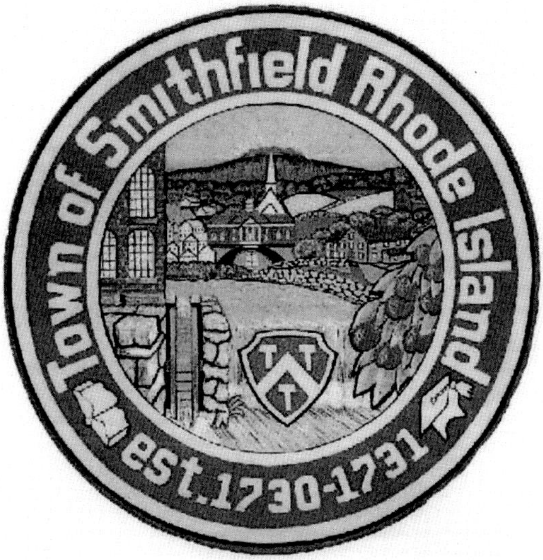

Smithfield's current town seal.

symbols ranging from animals, tools and weapons to moons and stars, and everything in between.

The hammer has always been a symbol of strength and industry. There are different opinions as to what the hammers on the town seal mean. One states that they are representative of the fact that Smithfield was divided into three towns in 1871. Others say that the hammers represent the virtues of Truth, Honor and Value. However, in recent years it has come to be commonly accepted that they represent the three main villages of the town, namely, Greenville, Georgiaville and Esmond, although this does not explain why Spragueville and Stillwater were overlooked. Perhaps all are correct and the meaning of the hammers has changed over time.

In 1997, a new town seal was adopted that included various symbols related to the town's history. The new seal proved unpopular, as many considered it "too busy," so it was replaced by the current town seal in 1999. However, the 1997 seal was still used by the planning office on plat map books as late as 2002.

The present Smithfield town seal was conceived by local artist Neil Sally. The popular seal represents Smithfield's mill and apple-growing industries, as well as a modernized version of the town's original seal. In the background, Wolf Hill can be seen, which many say divides the town both geographically and politically. Also included are the town hall, the Greenville Baptist Church and the Smith-Appleby House, which is Smithfield's oldest building.

Chapter 4
Village Settlement

According to the book *The History of the State of Rhode Island and Providence Plantations*, published in 1920 by Thomas Williams Bicknell, land was settled on "Wyonkeag Hill," today spelled "Wionkhiege Hill," as early as 1667 or 1670.

The name is pronounced Wine-a-Keeg and is said to be Native American in origin. Legend has it that at one time there was a small garrison posted there that kept kegs of wine in lieu of drinking water. Local Native Americans would come to trade for the kegs, and thus they named the hill Wionkhiege Hill, meaning Wine Keg Hill. True or not, it makes for an interesting legend.

We tend to think of water in those days as being clean and pure, but such was not always the case. In fact, waterborne diseases were a major health hazard until the days of modern chlorinated drinking water. Therefore, many people in early America drank beer, wine, cider and tea.

The Smithfield of today is a town made up of five main villages: Greenville, Stillwater, Esmond, Spragueville and Georgiaville. It is interesting to note that the villages of Greenville, Esmond and Stillwater were all settled before 1730, while Smithfield was still part of the town of Providence.

Greenville

The oldest of Smithfield's five villages is Greenville, first settled in 1685 by Joshua Winsor, who established the first mill there. The original name of the settlement, if in fact it had one, has been lost to history, for the name Greenville wasn't given to the area until after the American Revolutionary War ended in 1785. The name was given in honor of Major General Nathanael Greene, who was a Rhode Island–born general who served under George Washington.

In 1689, Resolved Waterman came to the area and later built the famous Waterman Tavern in 1733. The tavern proved to be a highly successful enterprise due to its location on Putnam Pike, which was a major travel route from Plymouth, Massachusetts, to upstate New York. The tavern remained in operation into the early twentieth century. Most of the building was demolished in 1936 to make way for the widening of Putnam Pike, and today, only the rear ell dating to the 1850s remains. As of this writing, members of the Smithfield Preservation Society are in the process of restoring the ell, which at one time also served as a bank.

One legend concerning the old Waterman Tavern comes from a high school essay written in 1929 by Miss Dorothy Whipple. The story tells of an anonymous traveler who stopped in one night with his pet rattlesnake. After a few drinks, the man produced the snake from a knapsack and announced that it could do tricks. At one point, the snake slithered into the huge stone fireplace that once graced the keeping room, and when the man went to retrieve it, the creature bit him with a lethal dose of venom. It is said that the mysterious traveler was buried in an unmarked grave somewhere on the outskirts of Greenville.

Another folktale relates how a guest of the tavern is said to have disappeared one night while sleeping in the basement. He was presumed to have fallen down an open well in the cellar, but his body was never recovered. His ghost was allegedly seen haunting the place for years afterward.

Exactly when these incidents are said to have occurred is unknown, but urban legends telling of mysterious lone travelers roaming highways and back roads, who appear at inns and hostels, date back two hundred years.

Another famous Greenville tavern was the one built by Thomas Paine in 1790, which stood where the Apple Valley Mall is located. Longtime residents will recall how in the 1940s, the Brown University mascot, a brown bear, was kept there in a cage behind the building. Elementary school field trips to pet and feed the bear were not uncommon.

The first church in Greenville was built by Baptists in 1701. It was later replaced by another Baptist church in 1821, which is still standing today, overlooking the Greenville Common. In early America, a church represented civilization and prosperity in a community. Travelers would look for the tall steeples in the distance to let them know that they were near a sizeable and civilized settlement.

Other early churches established in Greenville are St. Thomas Episcopal Church, 1851, and St. Phillip's Catholic Church, 1852.

Some may have heard of a place called "Knightsville" and wondered why the village is not found on any maps. That is because Knightsville was not a place, but a mill. In the 1840s, Stephen Rand, Albert Winsor and William F. Brown built a stone mill on Putnam Pike near Battey Drive, the remains of which can still be found today. In 1857, they sold it to Jeremiah Knight, who named it the Knightsville Mill.

Most of the earliest mills in Smithfield were saw- and gristmills. However, the beginning of the nineteenth century brought the proliferation of cotton mills to the area. Another early mill in Greenville was the Pooke & Steere Woolen Mill, later known as the Greenville Finishing Company, which closed in the 1970s. Today it is home to a variety of businesses, including an antique center.

There is a building across from the old Greenville Finishing Mill that has been called "the long house" over the years due to its being, well, long. It is said that the house was originally used as a pest house or sick house, where people afflicted with smallpox would be kept during an outbreak to prevent the spread of the disease. In later years, it served as an apartment house for millworkers.

Another Greenville mill was the Greenville Manufacturing Company, later occupied by the Stillwater Worsted Company, located on Austin Avenue at River Street. The mill was converted to housing about 1990.

Large mills required a good water supply to run the machinery during the dry summer months. Therefore, several Greenville reservoirs were constructed to store water for the mills. One of the first reservoirs to be created was the Slack's Reservoir in 1823. The following year the Woonasquatucket River Company was chartered under the Rhode Island General Assembly for the creation of other reservoirs in town. As a result, the Lower Sprague Reservoir was created in 1827; the Upper Sprague Reservoir in 1836; and Waterman's Reservoir in 1838.

Perhaps the earliest actual school in Greenville was the Smithfield Academy, built about 1810 on Austin Avenue near the present-day Greenville Post Office. Prior to its construction, children of Greenville were taught in a back room of the Waterman Tavern, something that would be considered unthinkable today. The academy building was replaced in 1874 by the Greenville School House, which stood at the same location. The schoolhouse remained in use until the William Winsor School was completed in 1930.

The old Greenville School was later used as a grange hall before being demolished to make way for a shopping center. All that remains of the old school is the bell, which currently sits on display at the Winfield Funeral Home.

One noteworthy resident of Greenville was Oscar A. Tobey, who served as Smithfield's town clerk for forty-five years, from 1871 until his death in 1917

Oscar Tobey's general store in Greenville also served as Greenville's post office. This photo, with Harold Tobey Smith standing in front of the store, dates to about 1917. The store was destroyed by fire on February 2, 1924. *Courtesy of Ralph W. Battey.*

at the age of eighty-one. No other town clerk in Rhode Island has held that position for that length of time before or since. Tobey administered his office from his general store in Greenville, and until Smithfield established the town hall in Georgiaville in 1921, all town records were kept in Tobey's store. Besides holding the office of town clerk, Tobey also served as Greenville's postmaster from 1882 until 1902.

Stillwater

The first to settle in Stillwater was Elisha Smith, who built the famous Smith-Appleby House about 1700. Elisha was the grandson of John Smith, one of the men who came to Rhode Island with Roger Williams in 1636. The house is believed to be the oldest in Smithfield and is said to be one of the oldest in the state. Elisha came from Providence to establish a farm and a mill and eventually acquired over seven hundred acres of land.

The Smith-Appleby House originated as a one-room stone-ender, meaning one end was constructed entirely of stone that contained a large open hearth. This was typical of early Rhode Island home construction. The house has seen several additions over the years, the last in the 1830s.

The last of the Smith-Appleby family line to live in the house was Maria Appleby, who came to Stillwater in 1905. Maria ran a successful dairy farm until the 1920s, when she sold off the dairy herd and established the Stillwater Country Club, which was Smithfield's one and only golf course. The golf course began with six holes but was later expanded to nine, and it existed where Interstate 295 presently passes over Stillwater Road. A barn on Stillwater Road served as a clubhouse where the seventy-five dues-paying members could refresh themselves or purchase golf equipment. The golf course remained in operation until the late 1950s, when it was sold to a Massachusetts couple who decided to close it.

Maria Appleby died in 1959, leaving the property to longtime companion, Abbie Sargeant, who passed away in 1963. Abbie willed the property to a church group that auctioned the contents of the house and left it vacant for many years. The house fell into disrepair and was in danger of being torn down until the Historical Society of Smithfield obtained it in 1976 and began a long-term restoration project. Today, the large, eighteen-room house is Smithfield's only museum and serves as the headquarters of the Historical

This picture of the Smith-Appleby House in Stillwater dates to about 1915. The house is the oldest structure in Smithfield. *Courtesy of the Historical Society of Smithfield.*

This building on Stillwater Road was built about 1870. Over the years it has served as a general store, a yarn shop, a meeting hall and a movie theatre. Today it serves as a day-care center.

Society of Smithfield. It is open to the public and visited by hundreds of people every year.

In 1824, a cotton mill was built in the area by Israel and Welcome Arnold. This mill was later destroyed by fire, as were all subsequent mills built on this spot. (For more information, see Chapter 8, "The Stillwater Mill Fire.")

Today, the village of Stillwater is a quiet residential area, but in the later 1800s and early 1900s, it boasted a large mill, blacksmith shop, railroad station, general store, movie hall, post office and schoolhouse.

The Stillwater schoolhouse was a two-and-a-half-story building on Stillwater Road near Hanton City Trail. Prior to its construction in 1869, local children were schooled in nearby homes.

Esmond

The village of Esmond was settled as early as 1703, when Major William Smith built a home there. However, Esmond wasn't the original name for the area. In fact, it appears that the area didn't have a name until after 1813, when Governor Phillip Allen bought land and erected a mill there. The mill was successful, and the governor was philanthropic, for in 1820 he built a combination schoolhouse and church for the local citizens. It was about this time that the area was named Allenville.

In January 1881, the name was changed to Enfield when the first post office was established. The name was changed to Esmond about 1906, when the Esmond Mills opened and began producing its famous blankets.

The blankets produced at Esmond Mills were known as "Esmond Bunny Blankets" and were regarded throughout the country for their high quality. The blankets bore the "Esmond Bunny" logo, which was a rabbit sitting up on its hind legs. As a means to market the blankets, the mill produced several editions of children's books relating the story of Bunny Esmond. The basic story related how poor Bunny Esmond is tricked by a sly fox that cuts off all his fur, but Bunny Esmond is kept warm by a nice Esmond blanket. Esmond Mills also reportedly made blankets for the U.S. Army during World War I.

Many mill villages were close-knit communities, and Esmond was no exception. During its heyday, the Esmond Mills sponsored sports teams and company outings for its employees. The mill even owned Esmond Park and

The Esmond Mill complex has been a fixture in Smithfield for over one hundred years. The brick mill seen today dates to 1906 and replaced an earlier one dating to the early 1800s that stood on the same location.

The Esmond Mill complex was self-sustaining. This view shows the mill carpentry shop, circa 1925. *Courtesy of Donald and Claire Mercier.*

employed a crew to maintain it. After World War I, the mill owners erected a monument at the corner of Waterman Avenue and Esmond Street to those from Esmond who served in the war.

Besides the school that was built by Governor Allen in 1820, another school existed on Chamberlain Street that is today a private residence. Yet another, built in 1849, existed on Esmond Street just beyond Maple Avenue. The old Dorothy T.P. Dame School, which opened in 1908, presently serves as the East Smithfield Public Library.

An interesting story about the old Dame School concerns a discovery made by workmen who were renovating the building for use as a library in January 1985. While removing some old blackboards, contractors found even older blackboards underneath with messages written in chalk by schoolchildren of the class of 1931.The writing looked as new as the day it was scrawled and included hand-drawn pictures of flowers and urns, as well as the individual names of children. After photographing the blackboards, it was decided to leave them as they were and cover them over with drywall. These "time capsules" of sorts still lie hidden behind the modern walls of the library until the day when future renovations might once again bring them to light.

The church built by Governor Allen remained in use into the 1880s. Any Protestant minister was allowed to hold services there; however, the church did not have a permanent minister assigned to it. The church was located on Esmond Street across from Maple Avenue.

SPRAGUEVILLE AND MOUNTAINDALE

Spragueville was first settled in 1733 by Abraham Smith, who constructed a small mill and two homes in the area. However, the area is named for James Sprague, who later erected a mill of his own.

Thomas Sprague built a cotton mill there in the 1820s and the business became known as T. Sprague & Sons, which was later sold to Wanton Vaughn in 1847 and renamed the Granite Mill Company.

Mountaindale was more or less a village within the village of Spragueville on the opposite side of Mountaindale Pond at the foot of Wolf Hill. A small factory was established there in the 1820s that produced machine items and parts for cotton looms. The business later became the Mountaindale Hosiery Mill, which remained in operation until about the 1890s.

Another business located in the area was the East Providence Ice Company, which had an icehouse on Mountaindale Road. Longtime area resident Charles Jaswell, age eighty-seven, related how he went to work for the ice company when he was fourteen years old and made thirty-five cents an hour. It was dangerous work, but for a boy used to making ten cents an hour on local apple farms it was good money.

Of course the work was seasonal, and the season began as early as November 20 and would last until early March. The ice would freeze up to eighteen inches thick, and in a good year, they could do up to four ice harvests.

Ice harvesting was done in a systematic manner. In the early days, a team of horses pulling an ice cutter would be brought onto the ice. The cutter would be set for a particular depth, and the horses would make successive passes in a grid pattern, cutting about two-thirds into the depth of the ice. The grid would be roughly thirty to forty feet square. The edge cuts would go all the way through the ice, thus creating a floating island of ice. Men and boys would line up along the edge with long poles and push the island toward shore where the icehouse was located. There, the ice would be cut into smaller blocks using ice saws and then pushed into a channel that had a conveyor belt at one end. The conveyor belt would bring the blocks into the icehouse, where other workers would stack them and pack them in sawdust to await the warm weather.

In later years, gasoline-powered ice cutters were used, making the work go much quicker.

Icehouses were constructed of double walls, with about twelve inches or more of sawdust packed in between. Thus the buildings acted like modern-day coolers and kept the ice frozen until it was needed. Come summertime, the ice would be sold to commercial vendors who would ship it all over the world. Locally, ice men delivered ice to homeowners and businesses via horse-drawn wagons.

Spragueville wasn't the only area where ice was harvested. In fact, almost every body of water of any substantial size had an icehouse nearby.

The East Providence Ice Company went out of business sometime during World War II, as did many others when modern refrigeration became available to the average household. Today, all traces of the icehouse are gone.

Spragueville never reached the industrial manufacturing output of other villages of the town, but what it lacked in industry, it made up for in apple orchards. In the early twentieth century, the area was covered with apple orchards and some considered it the heart of Apple Valley. (For more information about Spragueville's apple orchards, see Chapter 7.)

Spragueville had a traditional one-room schoolhouse that was located on Swan Road a short distance up from Pleasant View Avenue. The building still exists today as a private residence.

Georgiaville

The village of Georgiaville can trace its origins to Thomas Owen, who was the first to settle there in 1752. Three years later, John Farnum came to the area and established an iron forge, where he produced iron products that he sold in Providence and Connecticut. He is responsible for having built the section of Farnum Pike that runs from Georgiaville to Providence to have a convenient means to take his iron to market. Upon his death in 1772, his sons, Joseph and Noah, continued their father's business.

On May 10, 1813, Joseph and Noah sold their mill rights to Samuel G. Arnold, Thomas Thompson and Samuel Nightingale, who constructed a cotton mill along the Woonasquatucket River. The mill was occupied by the Georgiaville Manufacturing Company, a company based in Georgia. It is said that the area was originally to be called Nightingale, but the name was changed to Georgiaville after the cotton company established itself there.

In 1828, the company built a second mill and added to it in 1846. Georgiaville Pond was created in 1853 to supply enough water to power the growing mill.

This circa 1920 view of Stillwater Road looking toward River Street shows several mill homes where those employed at the Bernon Mill lived. *Courtesy of the Historical Society of Smithfield.*

The Georgiaville Mill was later purchased by the Bernon Company, which remained in operation into the twentieth century. The company was responsible for establishing a library and a fire company. (For more information about the Georgiaville Fire Company, see Chapter 8.) The complex later became home to the Industrial Tool Company, which remained in operation until the early 1980s. Today the mill is occupied by condominiums and town houses and is known as Homestead Mills.

In 1840, Noah Farnum built the Georgiaville Tavern on Farnum Pike on the corner of Wolf Hill Road. For many years the tavern served as a rest stop for the stagecoaches that once ran from Providence to Massachusetts. Today, it is a private residence.

Perhaps the first church in Georgiaville was the Georgiaville Baptist Church, established in 1857. The original church stood until 1906 where the parking lot of the Georgiaville Beach is today. The church was replaced by a new one on Farnum Pike in 1906. Other churches included St. Michael's Catholic Church, established in 1875, and the Universalist church, established in 1888.

There is a statue of St. Michael the Archangel that sits atop a small hill overlooking the parking lot of the present St. Michael's Church on Farnum Pike. It was made for a Providence order of Franciscan nuns in the 1950s and was abandoned when they moved to new quarters a few years later. In 1990, it was discovered by a Providence arson investigator who thought it would

The Georgiaville Pharmacy was located on Farnum Pike and is today a private residence. *Courtesy of Donald and Claire Mercier.*

be a nice addition to St. Michael's in Georgiaville. After some negotiations, the statue was purchased, brought to Smithfield and restored. The unveiling ceremony took place on September 29, 1991.

The Universalist church was built on Farnum Pike in 1888 and still stands today; however, it has gone through extensive remodeling over the years. At one point, a fire destroyed the upper half of the structure. After serving as a church, the building was used as Smithfield's town hall from 1921 to 1939, before the present town hall was constructed. Today, the building serves as a VFW post.

Many will not be pleased to learn that during the 1920s, Ku Klux Klan rallies were held in Georgiaville in an area then known as Klan Field, which was located near Potter Avenue. The participants were Klan members belonging to the Providence chapter who held rallies in rural areas of the state—not just in Smithfield. It is said that Stillwater Road would become grid-locked with cars as people came from as far away as Massachusetts and Connecticut to watch or participate.

In 1927, leaders of the Klan hatched a plot to take over the First Light Infantry of the Rhode Island Militia by advising all members to enlist in the hopes of curtailing state interference of Klan activities. The plan failed when a Greenville Klan member came forward and alerted state officials.

The first school in Georgiaville was built in 1850 on present-day School Street. It served the children of Georgiaville until 1923, when the Irving S. Cook School was built on Farnum Pike. Today the old Cook School serves as the School Department's administrative building.

The old Georgiaville School continued its life as a fire station from 1924 to 1942. It then served as a town highway garage until it became too costly to maintain. Ironically, it was burned as part of a training exercise by the fire department on May 8, 1961.

CHAPTER 5

THE TOWN POOR FARM AND ASYLUM

One of the darker chapters in the history of Smithfield concerns the town poor farm and asylum that once stood on Douglas Pike, a few rods north of Lydia Ann Road where the entrance to an industrial park is today. Between 1835 and 1871, the town's indigent and insane were sent there, sometimes willingly, other times not. The paupers' cemetery, with its anonymous fieldstone markers, is mute testimony that some never left.

Since its incorporation, the town of Smithfield has had its poor. In the eighteenth century, those unable to support themselves were on their own, as there were no social welfare programs in existence. Indigent persons were sometimes "sent away" lest they become a burden on the town. If they returned, they could be brought before the town council and fined or whipped. However, by the nineteenth century, attitudes had softened, and poor farms were established in many Rhode Island communities, Smithfield being one of them.

ESTABLISHING THE POOR FARM

In 1834, it was decided at a town meeting that Smithfield should look for a suitable location for a poor farm. In the 1830s, Smithfield was composed of the present-day municipalities of Lincoln, North Smithfield, Central Falls and a portion of Woonsocket. The farm needed to be in a centralized location that was also somewhat out of the way. The two-hundred-acre Seth Mowry Farm on Douglas Pike seemed to fit the bill. The following year, the town purchased the Mowry Farm for $5,500, and construction began soon afterward.

The idea behind the farm was to allow those in financial difficulty to have a place to go where they could have a roof over their heads until their

This 1991 photo shows the house and barn that once stood where the entrance to an industrial park is located today. This was the site of the Smithfield Poor Farm and Asylum, which operated from 1835 to 1871.

circumstances improved. To earn their keep, they were required to work in the fields, where they grew their own food.

The institution was administered by a keeper of the asylum, who in turn answered to an overseer of the poor, who in turn answered to a Board of Commissioners, which was appointed by the town.

Those who went to the farm were generally single mothers without any means of support, the elderly or disabled or those simply down on their luck. The 1850 federal census indicates that thirty-one women and children resided at the poor farm that year.

Going to the poor farm was a last resort. Nobody wanted to be there if they could help it. Besides the stigma, the place wasn't healthy. A common cause of death at the farm was consumption, which today we call tuberculosis. In the 1800s, it was almost always fatal.

Dying at the town farm meant an anonymous burial at the farm cemetery. The graves are marked with simple granite fieldstones set into the ground that bear no inscription to indicate who is buried there. At one time there were some who believed that these graves were Native American, but this has since been proven not to be the case.

The cemetery has a modern polished granite stone bench, which indicates that the first burial took place in 1838 and the last in 1880. Judging by the small number of headstones, and the fact that the farm was in operation for almost forty-five years, it seems probable that there are other graves that aren't marked at all.

In 1854, it was decided that a town asylum should be constructed at the town farm where those deemed mentally ill could be housed. The work was completed within a year.

The poor farm cemetery, designated as Smithfield Historical Cemetery #101, sits amidst a cusp of trees at the top of a hill overlooking Douglas Pike.

A SCANDAL IS BROUGHT TO LIGHT

Conditions at the town farm and asylum were less than ideal. Over time, rumors about events said to have happened at these institutions began to circulate, and some of the rumors, if true, were enough to shock the conscience.

The issue was raised at a town meeting held in June 1870. Exactly who brought up the subject is unknown, but part of the discussion focused on a man named James A——, whom, it was alleged, had been brought to the asylum in a "clandestine manner" and his care was so inadequate that his condition had worsened. Furthermore, he was allegedly being held in a cell in a perpetual state of nudity. After some discussion, it was decided that James should be transferred to the Worcester Insane Hospital since Butler Hospital in Providence was overcrowded.

It was also decided that an investigation should be conducted into the affairs of the town farm and asylum. There the matter seems to have rested. The summer of 1870 passed into autumn, and whatever investigation took place, if any, is not recorded.

Rumors persisted, leading one man to believe that something more needed to be done. On October 5, 1870, he took it upon himself to write an anonymous letter to the *Providence Journal*, which was printed on October 24, 1870. He signed the letter "Humanity." The letter cited certain instances of abuse, alleging "cruel, and barbarous treatment" of the inmates and dereliction of duty by those in charge or connected with the institutions.

The letter was apparently prompted by two recent events that the writer outlined. The first involved the case of a thirteen year-old girl named Nancy M——, whom, it was alleged, starved to death on September 11, 1870, because the overseer of the poor only gave Nancy's mother and two siblings fifty cents a week to live on. The family was allowed to live in a house off-site from the institutions that "Humanity" described as "miserable."

The second event was said to have occurred on October 12, 1870, when a pregnant seventeen-year-old girl named Susan T—— was brought to the farm at 2:00 a.m. by William M——, a man with whom she was living. They arrived in a buckboard wagon, and Susan had given birth while en route; however, the baby was stillborn. The keeper of the asylum, George R. Weaver, and his wife found the dead infant in the wagon with bruises on its body, which indicated to them that the death was caused by neglect or violence.

Susan was admitted to the farm under a written order from the overseer of the poor requiring the keeper to receive her whenever she should arrive and discharge her whenever she should wish to leave. According to "Humanity," when the keeper's wife demanded to know why Susan hadn't been brought to the institution sooner, rather than waiting until she was in labor, she was allegedly told that the overseer of the poor had specifically stated not to bring her until the last moment.

Mr. Weaver contacted Dr. N——, the institution physician, and demanded an inquest into the death of the baby. After examining the baby, the doctor felt an inquest was unnecessary, and "Humanity" quoted him as saying, "I've seen worse things than this done here."

The baby was buried in an unmarked grave in the town farm cemetery (Smithfield Historical Cemetery #101), and several days later, Susan went home with William M——.

"Humanity" went on to outline further allegations, citing a case in which a former keeper had allegedly slapped an elderly woman because "she didn't knit fast enough to suit him." "Humanity" also mentioned the case of an inmate named Melvina B——, whom he described as "once wealthy, and refined, and educated" but who was now disabled and unable to move about without assistance. She had requested a wheelchair but was allegedly told by the Board of Commissioners that the town was "too poor to afford her that luxury!" "Humanity" also alleged that the inmates' beds were old and infested with lice and vermin, indicating that they should be replaced. (Bedbugs and body lice were a common problem in the 1800s and were difficult to get rid of.)

"Humanity" wanted it to be clear that he did not fault the present keeper of the asylum, George Weaver, who had taken the position on April 1, 1870, and went on to praise Weaver and his qualifications. He then added that Weaver had not been paid his salary by the Board of Commissioners or given money for operating expenses, and since July 1, Weaver had been running the establishments on credit or at his own expense. The letter went on to state that in addition to everything else, Weaver had been informed by the commissioners that his services would no longer be needed as his predecessor had been rehired for the position. "Humanity" alleged that the reasons for Weaver's dismissal were "vague," "frivolous" and "trumped up." The specific charges against Weaver weren't listed in the *Providence Journal*, but it was said that he intended to fight all of them.

Apparently, part of the dispute between Weaver and the town was over conducting religious services at the institution. Weaver and his wife wanted to hold religious services and hopefully have a chapel built on the grounds. "Humanity" indicated that the Weavers had been promised a chapel would be built, but nothing had materialized so far.

THE INVESTIGATION

Things happened fast after the letter appeared, as Smithfield was suddenly thrust into the arena of public opinion. The following day, October 25, a special town meeting was called, where it was decided that a committee of five men should be appointed to investigate the allegations and their findings would be published in pamphlet form as well as in the *Providence Journal*. Those assigned to the investigation committee were all well known and respected members of the community.

If such allegations were made today, undoubtedly the investigation would be conducted by an outside law enforcement agency with no direct ties to the town. However, these were different times, when no such protocols were in place. Even if there had been, the Rhode Island State Police didn't come into existence until 1925. The Smithfield Police Department as we know it today didn't exist. In 1870, law enforcement in Smithfield consisted of an elected town sergeant and fourteen constables who were appointed by the town council. The only outside law enforcement agency at that time that could have had jurisdiction over the investigation was the Providence County Sheriff's Office; however, there is no indication that any law enforcement personnel or officers of the court were involved in the investigation. Therefore, it seems that the town essentially investigated itself.

On October 29, the Investigation Committee held its first meeting at the town farm to inspect conditions at the institution.

On October 30, 1870, the *Woonsocket Patriot* revealed that "Humanity," the pen name signed to the *Providence Journal* letter, was actually Colonel W.H. Walcott of Smithfield.

At a meeting held November 1, George Weaver, represented by Colonel Walcott, presented a bill to the town council asserting that he had not been paid by the Board of Commissioners for his previous six months of service. The council rejected the bill, stating it was a matter for the Board of Commissioners.

On November 11, the *Woonsocket Patriot* reported that the Investigation Committee had held three more meetings at the institution where witness testimony was gathered. It was further reported that the institution now had new iron beds to replace the old ones.

On November 29, 1870, the results of the investigation were released and published in an eleven-page pamphlet entitled, *Report of the Committee of Investigation on Charges Against the Overseer of the Poor, Commissioners of the Town Asylum, Keeper of the Town Asylum, and general treatment of the Poor in the Town Asylum.* Copies of this report have survived to this day, and excerpts of this public document are included in this chapter.

The Investigation Committee's Findings

The Investigation Committee's report dealt with each of Colonel Walcott's allegations separately.

Regarding the first charge relating to "cruel and barbarous treatment" of the inmates, the committee concluded that besides an "occasional lack of judgment in the treatment of the inmates, there has been no vicious use of authority or power," adding that "no cruel or barbarous treatment has been shown."

The second charge addressed by the report concerned the case of James A——, the inmate alleged to have been brought to the asylum in a "clandestine manner" and confined in a cell in a perpetual state of nudity. According to the report, the overseer of the poor had tried to place Mr. A—— in two other institutions but had been unable, so Mr. A—— was brought to Smithfield. The overseer reported that Mr. A—— had arrived at the town asylum around ten or eleven o'clock at night and had been placed in a room where he had stayed on a previous occasion.

The committee found that Mr. A—— should have been taken to an asylum in Worcester, Massachusetts, as it was its opinion that town asylums were not the best places to house insane persons. It was noted by the committee that the overseer had not taken Mr. A—— to Worcester due to a question of legal liability and fear of expense to the town. Therefore, the committee absolved the overseer of any wrongdoing.

The third charge related to the case of Nancy M——, who allegedly died of starvation. Nancy and her family had been living in a house provided by the overseer of the poor and given fifty cents per week to live on. To this the report stated: "These appear to have been permitted to live apart from that benign institution, the Asylum, in a miserable house provided for them by the Overseer. It may be that it was calculated the poor, wretched family would be able to eke out an existence on these small means, together with what they might earn by begging."

The house Nancy and her family lived in is described by the committee as "miserable," which begs the questions as to why they were permitted to live there and who owned the house? These questions are not addressed in the report. Furthermore, it was evidently felt that fifty cents a week was adequate because the "wretched family" could always go out and beg to earn more! It would seem that the whole reason for the town farm in the first place was so that people would not have to beg.

As to Nancy's death, the report states: "Poor Nancy over ate herself—on wild grapes—and sickened and died. Dr. N—— says that this child contracted a disease resembling the black vomit; and that nothing but grapes appeared to come from the stomach; and the mother says that the child subsisted on grapes for the last few days of her life, although the mother would hardly be willing to believe that her child died of starvation."

The Investigation Committee included what is reported to be the testimony of Nancy's mother and that of Dr. N——. It is not presented in a transcribed format, but rather paraphrased by the committee. They wrote: "It is due to the importance of this charge that the testimony in regard to it should be submitted by the Committee in so full a manner as that every freeman of the town shall be able to judge for himself whether or not the undersigned have come to a correct conclusion in regard to it."

What was presented as Nancy's mother's testimony is given in its entirety as follows:

> *The mother of Nancy M—— testified that at her solicitation the Overseer allowed Nancy, who was at the Asylum, to live with her, she being supported in part by the town. The Overseer paid the rent. Nancy was born with a spinal complaint, and had never been well; in her last sickness she had the gravel, and consumption. Mother and daughter went to house keeping in July. There was another child, then with them, and one born in August. The mother had other children who aided in her support. She testified that the Overseer gave her all she asked for. After Nancy was taken sick, the Overseer was accustomed to look in once a week and ask if she had things*

> *comfortable, to which both mother and daughter replied in the affirmative. The mother did not deem Nancy dangerously ill, until a very few days before her decease. She said, "We had all the fruit we wanted on the place. My daughter did not die of starvation. She had enough to eat, but did not tell the Overseer what she especially craved. She wanted eggs and meat. I did not tell the Overseer that she craved meat."*

There are several reasons why Nancy's mother would want her daughter to come and live with her even though she and the rest of the family were barely getting by. One could be that the asylum was no place for a young girl entering puberty. Another could be that the mother would need help with the arrival of the new baby in August, or possibly she just wanted the family to be together.

The report does not list a cause of death for Nancy, and perhaps the cause was not known. It could have been consumption, but black vomit is also a symptom of yellow fever, either of which could have been fatal in the nineteenth century. There does not seem to be any death record on file for Nancy at either the Central Falls City Hall or the Smithfield Town Hall.

One could surmise that Nancy's mother was in a tough situation following her daughter's death. There she was, with a new baby and another child to care for, no husband and no visible means of support, giving testimony in front of the very people whom she was reliant on for a home and support.

Dr. N——'s testimony was presented in a different fashion, as follows:

> *Dr. N——, is the physician connected with the asylum and has been for many years. Attended Nancy M—— in her last illness. She had spinal disease from birth. Vomited a black substance like black vomit. Knew nothing about her food when sick. Her mother was a very poor nurse. There was nothing in her case to indicate what food she had, and she made no complaint about her food. Diet would not produce the black vomit; want of food would not produce it. Saw the matter Nancy threw up. Saw no grapes. Did not say that nothing but grapes came from her stomach. The grape story belongs to other parties. I said nothing about it. Visited Nancy M—— as often as I judged, as a physician, it was necessary.*

The investigation committee concluded that there was no responsibility on the part of the town or those connected to the institutions for Nancy's death.

The next charge that the investigation report addressed concerned the case of Susan T—— and her deceased baby. Testimony from Mr. Weaver reiterated what had already been written in the *Providence Journal*. It does not appear that Mrs. Weaver gave any testimony.

The man who brought Susan to the town farm testified that he was told by the overseer to take her to the farm when he saw fit, adding that she didn't want to go to the farm and he only took her when she asked to go.

The overseer of the poor gave testimony that was condensed into only two sentences: "Gave William M—— an order to take Susan T—— to the town asylum; did not give him verbal instructions to wait till the last minute. Urged Susan to go to the asylum in July, but she declined to go believing that the father of the child would support her."

The identity of the father of Susan's child was never established in any official record, as no birth or death certificates for the child seem to exist in old town records. No testimony from Susan appears anywhere in the official Investigation Committee's report. There is, however, a statement from Dr. N—— concerning Susan and her baby:

> *Weaver, the keeper of the asylum, came after me; he thought the child had been murdered. I came up to the asylum with that idea in mind. The child was not murdered, and my feelings were relieved. I said "I have seen worse things than this," but did not say nor mean that I had seen worse things "done here." I was surprised. Did not think an inquest necessary. Did not think there was any violence. Child was still-born. The mother had been dreadfully kicked and pounded, about a month before the child was born, as she said, and she had felt no motion of the child since that time. This was before she went to W——'s. Decomposition had been going on two weeks or more before the child was born. My remark was made to relieve Mrs. Weavers mind.*

The committee's finding in this matter states simply that the overseer should not have left Susan in the care of another when it was the town's responsibility to care for her, but no indictment against the overseer was made. There is no mention in the investigation report of any criminal charges against whoever allegedly assaulted Susan and possibly caused the death of her baby.

As to the matter of the lack of religious services at the town farm, the Investigation Committee noted that they had never been held regularly despite the recommendation of the overseer and the commissioners, and admitted that no steps had been taken to ensure that they be held.

With regard to providing a wheelchair to Melvina B——, the report stated, "We think that although a better one than that provided would have been no more than the town would gladly have purchased, yet it is not a matter of the gravest importance." This sentence is difficult to interpret, but it doesn't look like Melvina got a wheelchair.

The next part of the report deals with the charges by the commissioners against the keeper, George Weaver. The charges listed against him are as follows:

1. The farm was not managed in a prudent and economical manner.
2. The inmates did their own cooking and table setting without supervision.
3. Mr. Weaver bought a stove without consulting any of the commissioners.
4. One field was turned out to meadow.
5. Wagons were left outside exposed to the elements.
6. The hay did not net the town what Mr. Weaver told the commissioners.
7. One cow was sold for less than he was directed to sell it for.
8. He has attempted to convert some goods of the inmates for his own use.

The Investigation Committee did not find merit in any of these charges.

As to Mr. Weaver's charges that the Board of Commissioners refused to sign purchase orders that he submitted, the Investigation Committee found that since Mr. Weaver had been able to operate the institutions by selling crops or on credit, the issue wasn't a problem. The committee concluded by stating, "We do not think that, in view of the accounts the town has paid, and is still responsible for, that in this regard he has any reason to complain."

In closing, the Investigation Committee concluded that those responsible for the town farm and asylum had acted in good faith, and other than the occasional lapse of good judgment, nobody had done anything wrong. It does not appear that anyone involved was prosecuted or disciplined as a result of the investigation.

On the final page of the investigation report, the committee noted that the town farm had not been a profitable venture for the town, nor was it likely to be. Therefore, the recommendation was made that it be sold.

The Aftermath

It appears that conditions at the institutions improved after the investigation, as it was noted in the *Woonsocket Patriot* on February 24, 1871, that the inmates had been served a turkey dinner for Washington's birthday.

George Weaver resigned as keeper on April 1, 1871, and was replaced by E.S. Harris. He did not plan on staying past April 1 anyway, so it may be assumed that he left by mutual agreement.

The rusting remains of this old piece of farm equipment can still be seen on what was once the Smithfield Poor Farm property.

On October 13, 1871, shortly after the division of the town had taken place, the *Woonsocket Patriot* reported that at a special town meeting it had been decided to sell the town farm and asylum at auction. The farm was being sold, it was said, not due to the scandal, but because it was no longer profitable. The overseers of the poor for the new towns of Lincoln and North Smithfield were notified to remove any residents from their towns now residing at the farm in Smithfield on or before January 1, 1872.

The Board of Commissioners was disbanded as there was no longer any need of it. Smithfield's overseer of the poor found a new job as overseer of the poor in North Smithfield. He died in 1877 at the age of sixty-three.

After the poor farm property was sold, it became a private dairy farm that remained in operation into the late twentieth century. The remnants of the farm were demolished in the 1990s to make way for a road that leads into an industrial park.

There will no doubt be some who feel this chapter of Smithfield's history should be deleted. There were probably those who felt that way in 1871. To quote the Roman philosopher Marcus Tullius Cicero, "The first law for the historian is that he shall never dare utter an untruth. The second is that he shall suppress nothing that is true."

CHAPTER 6

WHEN SMITHFIELD HAD RAILROADS

Along Farnum Pike, if one takes the time to notice, one will see the remains of old rail beds that once carried trains as they rumbled through town on their way to Providence or Massachusetts. The tracks, abandoned in the 1960s and later torn up, belonged to four railroad companies over the years, the last being the New York, New Haven & Hartford Rail Road.

Today, one may wonder why Smithfield needed or even wanted a railroad. If it were suggested that one be built today, it would likely be vehemently opposed with the "not in my backyard" attitude. As proof, one may remember that back in the 1990s, many people were opposed to turning the old rail beds into a bike path. However, the fact is, people of the town wanted and needed the railroad. It provided cheap transportation of goods and people, and aided the local economy. With this in mind, one may question why the railroad was abandoned.

THE BEGINNING

Railroads were in operation in Rhode Island as early as 1835. These were main lines running between large cities such as Providence, Boston, Hartford and Worcester, with depots in any village or town that happened to be along the route. Branch lines to other areas came later, primarily as a way to connect one main line to another.

The Providence and Worcester Railroad, chartered in 1844, was the first railroad to come through Smithfield. The tracks were opened on October 27, 1847, and ran along the northern border of the town in what is today Lincoln, North Smithfield and Woonsocket, through the villages of Albion, Manville, Bernon and Waterford. When the division of Smithfield occurred in 1871, Smithfield, as we know it today, was without a railroad, but not for

These wood timbers are all that remain of a railroad bridge that crossed the Woonasquatucket River just north of present-day Rogler Farm Road.

long. The process to build another railroad began with the application for a charter renewal of the Woonasquatucket Railroad Company.

The Woonasquatucket Railroad first obtained its charter by an act of the Rhode Island General Assembly in January 1857, with the intent of building a rail line that would follow the Woonasquatucket River from Providence all the way to the Massachusetts state line. Unfortunately, financial setbacks, followed by the Civil War, delayed the start of the project. The charter was eventually renewed in 1872.

The first rail lines opened in present-day Smithfield on Monday, August 11, 1873. However, long before any track was laid, there had been much debate as to where the rails should go. The only thing that everyone agreed upon was that those living in the "north country," which included all of the towns in northwest Rhode Island, wanted the railroad to come to them.

Newspapers of the era carried articles of the debate. It seemed that every mill owner wanted the tracks to run directly past his mill; every farmer hoped they would pass near his farm; and every village wanted a depot. The debate lasted nearly three years before a final decision was made.

On November 20, 1871, a meeting was held in Greenville to discuss the possibility of the Woonasquatucket Railroad laying tracks that would connect the villages of Greenville, North Scituate and Chepachet. The meeting was attended by prominent citizens of each town who debated the cost and construction of two proposed routes. One proposal, termed "the North Route," would run from Providence to Stillwater, then directly to Pascoag, and would cost $862,061. The other route would run from Providence to Greenville, to North Scituate and Chepachet, and was estimated to cost $1,108,716. Naturally it was hoped that the railroad would approve the more expensive option, but it was feared that the businessmen in the northern communities might exert their influence to have the less expensive route constructed.

It was concluded that the longer route might be more readily accepted if the towns of Smithfield, Scituate and Glocester could raise cash subscriptions totaling $150,000 to offset the difference in cost. Each town appointed a committee charged with raising the money.

By March 1872, exactly where to locate the rail lines was still in debate, but now that the Woonasquatucket Railroad Company had received a renewal of its charter, things began to move quickly. Despite the formation of the fundraising committees in Smithfield, Scituate and Glocester, the railroad went ahead with plans to build the northern route to Pascoag.

On March 15, 1872, the *Woonsocket Patriot* announced the appointment of officers of the newly reincorporated Woonasquatucket Railroad Company. William Tinkham was named president; L.M.E. Stone as chief engineer and treasurer; and Henry C. Clark as secretary. The board of directors included William Tinkham, Edward Pearce, M.B.I. Goodard, H.C. Clark, A.L. Sayles, A.N. Beckwith, L.M.E. Stone, H.A. Kimball and James O. Inman.

On April 5, 1872, it was announced that the northern route would be planned as soon as weather would permit. By the middle of April, the proposed line was laid out on paper, and by June construction was well underway.

Sometime between March and June, the name of the railroad was changed from the Woonasquatucket Railroad to the Providence and Springfield Railroad. The reason for the name change is unclear at this time, but most likely it was because the company had ambitions of extending the line all the way to Springfield, Massachusetts.

Branch Lines

The decision to run the tracks to Pascoag led the citizens of Greenville to propose that a branch line be run from Stillwater to Greenville at an estimated cost of $70,000—$30,000 of which would have to be raised by stock subscriptions. A meeting was held in January 1873 and a resolution was passed. Many were in favor of this project, including residents of Scituate who hoped to eventually connect to the Greenville Branch.

On March 7, 1873, the *Woonsocket Patriot* reported that of the $30,000 in stock required, $19,000 had been subscripted so far. The paper further reported that the Town of Smithfield would be required to take out $40,000 in bonds to make up the $70,000. On March 28, it was reported that $20,500 had been raised.

Construction of the Greenville Branch looked promising, but there were some who opposed it. The reasons why can only be speculated at this time because they were not recorded. Perhaps some people didn't want a train passing near or on their residential property. Perhaps some had a vested interest in the stagecoach lines that ran from Providence through Greenville to Burrillville. Whatever the reasons, a special town meeting was held in Georgiaville on May 20, 1873, to vote on the matter. The issue was whether the town should take out the $40,000 in bonds to build the branch line. The *Woonsocket Patriot* reported that there were 226 qualified electors to vote on the question and 195 showed up to vote. The results were 83 in favor, 112 against, and there the matter lay for the time being.

In the meantime, construction on the Providence to Pascoag Line continued at a rapid pace. By early May 1873, it was announced that the rails had been laid from Providence to Dyerville, and that they were expected to reach Pascoag by July. The July deadline proved to be accurate.

On Monday, August 11, 1873, the first passenger train ran along the new twenty-two-mile railroad. The train consisted of three cars, which were reportedly "well filled."

On August 16, about two hundred citizens of Pascoag boarded the train and traveled by rail all the way to Rocky Point in Warwick. The day-trippers were entertained along the way by the Pascoag Cornet Band. Before the railroad, a trip such as this would have been long and difficult.

With the opening of the new railroad, there was renewed interest in construction of the Greenville Branch. Even though the voters had rejected the idea, subscriptions were still being sold, and by the middle of May, the entire $30,000 had been raised.

On May 19, a special town meeting was held to conduct another vote on the matter. This time the results were 99 in favor, 55 against. One can only guess what changed voters' minds, but the matter now seemed resolved in favor of constructing the Greenville Branch.

A site survey conducted in January 1874 laid out two possible routes for the branch line. The first would place the tracks close to the woolen mill of Sterry Whipple, and intersect Putnam Pike a few hundred feet west of Austin Avenue near the home of Daniel Garey. The second route would have crossed Log Road and intersected Putnam Pike a little farther to the west, necessitating the construction of a large bridge so the tracks could cross a millpond. This route would have put the tracks closer to the Knightsville and Pooke and Steere Mills. Cost estimates for both routes ranged from

$43,000 to $60,000, with an additional $14,000 required to construct the bridge across the millpond.

On May 25, 1874, a special meeting of the Board of Directors of the Providence and Springfield Railroad was held to consider the matter, but the recent death of one of the directors prevented any formal action from being taken. Another meeting was scheduled for February 1875.

By the spring of 1875, the matter was still unresolved. What happened isn't clear, but a news item printed in the *Woonsocket Patriot* on April 30, 1875, indicates that the Board of Directors was no longer interested in building the Greenville Branch. The article went on to state that the citizens of Greenville planned to petition the Ponagansett Railroad Company to construct the branch line.

Apparently, the Ponagansett Railroad never built the Greenville Branch, or any other line. There were many investors trying to obtain charters for railroads at the time, and although a few charters were granted, some railroads only existed on paper. The Greenville Branch was never built, and this was the end of the matter.

By 1878, the Providence and Springfield Railroad was running three locomotives, three passenger cars and seventy-seven freight cars along the Smithfield route, and business was good. People could now travel from Smithfield to Burrillville or Providence in less time than it would take to ride a horse from one side of town to the other, and the railroad was certainly quicker and more comfortable than traveling by stagecoach.

In 1890, the Providence and Springfield Railroad changed its name to the New York & New England Railroad. In 1895, the name changed again to the New England Rail Road.

In 1898, the tracks were taken over by the New York, New Haven & Hartford Rail Road, which was chartered in 1872 by a merger between the New York/New Haven Rail Road and the New Haven & Hartford Rail Road. At its peak in 1929, the railroad owned 2,131 miles of track in Rhode Island, Connecticut, Massachusetts and New York.

The New York, New Haven & Hartford Rail Road continued to operate in Smithfield until 1962.

Railroad Routes

Along the tracks were railroad stations, some large and some small, but all tended to be gathering places for locals eager to socialize and catch the latest news.

The tracks began in Providence, with stations at Dike Street, Olneyville, Dyerville, Manton, Lymansville, Allendale, Centerdale and Greystone, before reaching Smithfield.

The rail line entered Smithfield via Esmond and ran behind the Esmond Mill complex where the Esmond Station was located. A spur ran off the main line to the mill for loading and unloading. The tracks continued north, where they crossed Esmond Street near Maple Avenue. At this spot, one can still see the old steel rails poking through the asphalt of Esmond Street.

From there they passed by Esmond Park and crossed over Farnum Pike at Leland Mowry Road, which at that time was known as the "Bull Run Crossing." Leland Mowry was the stationmaster of the Esmond station in the early 1900s and the road is named for him. This portion of the rail bed still survives as a walking trail.

In Georgiaville, the tracks cut across Higgins Street and Homestead Avenue, past the Georgiaville station and then on to Whipple Avenue and Stillwater Road, where they continued north between Farnum Pike and the west side of Georgiaville Pond. In this area, there was another spur leading to the Bernon Mill, which is now known as the Homestead Mill condominiums.

Past Georgiaville Pond, the tracks continued north to Capron Road. The Stillwater station was located on the south side of Capron Road at this crossing.

Anecdotal reports say that there was also a water tower here where the engine could take on water to keep the boiler cool. Boiler explosions were a real danger in the days when steam locomotives were in use.

North of Capron Road, the tracks followed the shoreline past Capron Pond and the Woonasquatucket River into Stillwater Village. This portion of the rail bed also survives today as a walking trail.

In Stillwater, there was another spur that ran in back of the Stillwater Mill. The Stillwater Mill was destroyed by fire in May 1984, but the stone buildings where the spur once ran up to are still in existence, although in very poor condition.

North of Stillwater, the line followed the Woonasquatucket River back to Farnum Pike, where it crossed over and paralleled the west side of the highway. It crossed over again near present-day Industrial Drive. From there it ran along the east side of Farnum Pike and crossed Brayton Road, where the Smithfield Station was located.

Beyond the Smithfield station, the line continued north until it approached the North Smithfield town line, where it turned to the east and crossed Douglas Pike at what was known as the "Douglas Crossing" and continued into North Smithfield. From there the line continued all the way into Douglas, Massachusetts, ending at Douglas Junction.

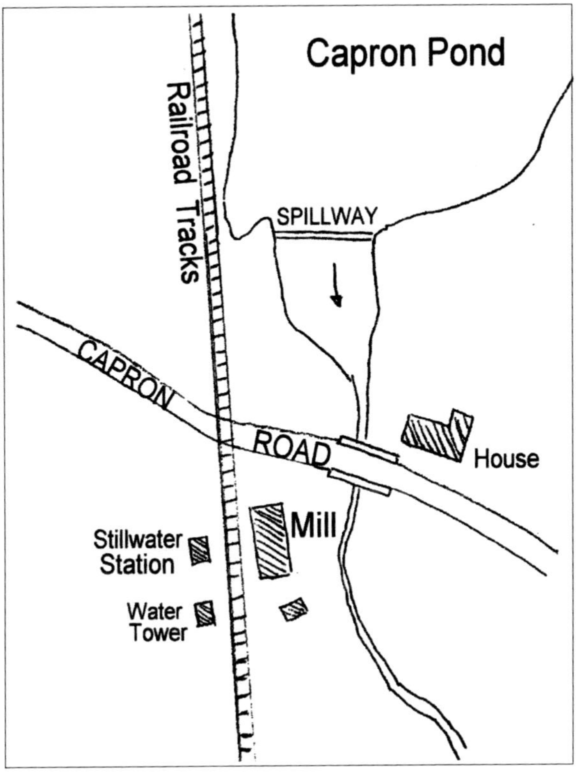

This illustration indicates where the Stillwater Station and other structures were located on Capron Road. Today, only the house remains.

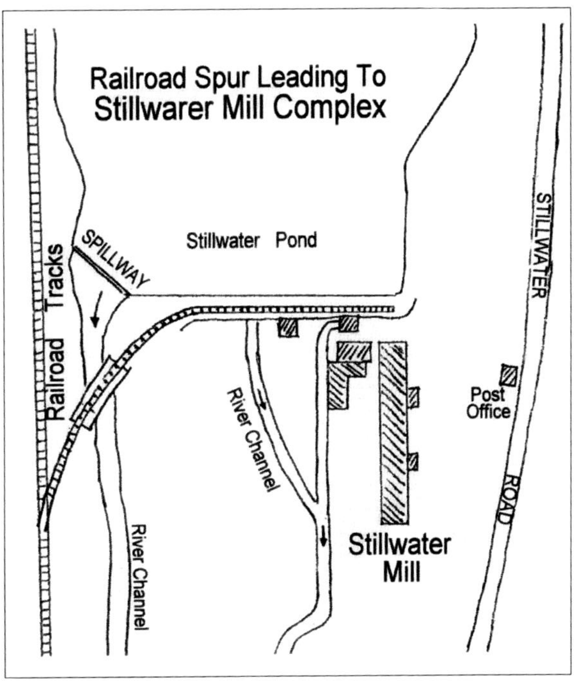

This illustration shows how a railroad spur ran to the Stillwater Mill.

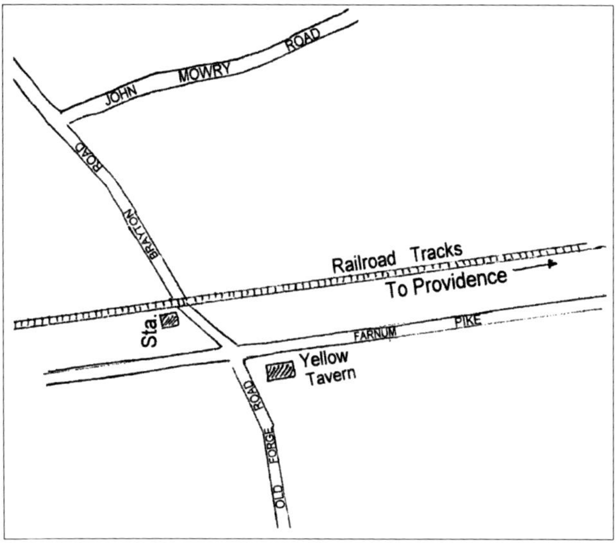

This illustration indicates the original location of the Smithfield Station on Brayton Road. The Smithfield Station is the only surviving railroad station in Smithfield.

This is the old Smithfield train station as it looked in 1975, before restoration. Today it can be viewed by the public at the Smith-Appleby House Museum. *Courtesy of the Historical Society of Smithfield.*

SMITHFIELD DEPOTS

There were four railroad stations in Smithfield: Esmond, Georgiaville, Stillwater and the Smithfield Station, located at the Brayton Avenue Crossing in the northern part of town. All were built in the 1870s, and of the four, only the Smithfield Station has survived.

The Smithfield Station was known as a flag stop, so called because if someone wanted the train to stop, they would hang a flag. If the train's engineer didn't see a flag, the train would pass by.

After the railroad abandoned passenger service in the early 1930s, the Smithfield Station fell into disrepair and was in danger of being torn down. In 1975, the Historical Society of Smithfield purchased the station for $300 and moved it to the Smith-Appleby House property. There it sat for almost five years until it was taken to the Davies Technical School in Lincoln to be restored as part of a community service project. In November 1980, it was returned to the Smith-Appleby House, where it was placed on display. Today, the public can examine this piece of the town's railroad history.

The Smithfield Station is small, only ten by thirteen feet, with an A-frame roof. Inside are two small rooms that make up a waiting area and an office. The waiting room has benches and a cast-iron stove that came from the Stillwater depot. The office served as a post office where the postmaster also sold penny candy and gum to local children.

Although most of the outside was replaced during restoration, the building still retains its original interior, left just as it was when the station closed. Looking along the walls, one can still see initials and dates carved into the woodwork by bored children awaiting the train. Some of the initials have dates next to them, ranging from 1911 to the 1920s.

The End of the Line

Just as the stagecoach lines lost passengers to the railroads, the railroads eventually lost passengers to the trolley, bus lines and the automobile. As a result, passenger service along the Providence to Pascoag run was discontinued in 1931.

The railroad continued to move freight up and down the line several times a day, but during the Great Depression profits fell off, and in 1937, the section of track running from Pascoag to Douglas, Massachusetts, was totally abandoned.

By the mid-1950s, many roads in northern Rhode Island were paved. This allowed trucking companies to better compete with the railroad for the transportation of goods from the mills. As a result, railroad profits fell and service was gradually cut. In 1962, the 19.3-mile stretch from Olneyville to Pascoag was abandoned. The remaining 1.4-mile portion between Providence and Olneyville closed in 1965.

Railroad Accidents

Nationally, railroad accidents happened frequently in the late 1800s and early 1900s. There are no known records documenting each and every railroad accident, but enough documentation has survived to prove that Smithfield wasn't immune. In fact, it seems that almost from the start there were safety concerns.

At a town council meeting held on January 29, 1876, the council was presented with a petition asking it to require the railroad to assign flagmen at the locations where the tracks crossed roadways in the town. Citizens cited several instances when they had experienced narrow escapes at some of the more dangerous crossings.

Whatever happened with the petition is not recorded. It can be surmised that the railroad was not anxious to incur the cost of flagmen, for if it did so in Smithfield, other towns would want flagmen too. There was also the question of whether the town had the legal authority to force the railroad to hire flagmen.

The first known railroad accident in Smithfield occurred at the Brayton Avenue Crossing on December 24, 1878, when a wagon hauling trash was struck by a train. The driver survived, but one of his horses did not. The driver claimed that he had no warning that the train was approaching.

Town death records show that the first railroad fatality in Smithfield happened on August 14, 1888, when a fifty-five-year-old man was struck and killed by a passing train. Another man was struck and killed on April 27, 1892. The exact location of these incidents is not recorded.

A wreck involving a head-on collision between two trains occurred about a mile north of Stillwater on June 12, 1894, when ten people were seriously injured. The accident was blamed on the telegraph operator at the Stillwater Station who improperly relayed instructions to the northbound train.

At that time, the railroad owned what was called a "wrecking train" that was kept in Providence. The train was a disaster response vehicle that would carry special equipment and work crews to clear the tracks, as well as medical staff to treat the injured. When word of the accident reached Providence, the "wrecking train" was immediately dispatched.

In November 1921, a forty-year-old man was hit while walking along the tracks, injuring his leg. The leg became infected and he died on December 3.

On May 16, 1924, a thirty-seven-year-old man was killed when he fell under the train as it passed through Stillwater.

Perhaps the worst accident occurred on April 14, 1925, when four people in an automobile were killed at the Douglas Crossing near the Smithfield/North Smithfield line.

Twenty years later, on September 18, 1945, another automobile was hit by a train at the Bull Run Crossing on Farnum Pike, killing one Smithfield resident and injuring six others.

On September 28, 1955, the Douglas Pike Crossing was once again the scene of a tragedy when a thirty-year-old man apparently didn't realize that a train was crossing and drove his car into the side of it, killing himself.

Trolley Lines—Smithfield's Other Railroads

Smithfield's other railroads were the trolley lines that operated from 1895 to 1935, which offered people the opportunity to get to places not serviced by the railroads.

The lines in Smithfield ran the length of Putnam Pike from Johnston to Glocester, and on Route 104, from North Providence to Esmond Street. The nice thing about trolleys was that they didn't require a long stopping distance like a train and, therefore, didn't use stations in the traditional sense. There were of course regular trolley stops, much like bus stops of today, yet in many cases, all one had to do was signal the conductor and the trolley would stop.

Most trolley cars had seats that could be reversed by flipping the backrest so that large groups could face one another during the ride or single riders could always face forward no matter which way the car was traveling.

The trolleys ran on electricity and were therefore quieter and cleaner than the noisy, smoke- and cinder-belching locomotives. In the summertime, open-sided cars offered a cooler ride than the trains.

Competition between the trolleys and the railroads was fierce. Trolley companies offered incentives, such as special day-time excursions to the country for city dwellers. Some companies even offered cemetery plots and a ride to the hereafter on a special funeral car. Others ran special coal and freight delivery trolleys. The railroads, in turn, made attempts to buy the trolley lines and put them out of business.

The trolley lines were run by a succession of companies over the years. Perhaps the best remembered is the United Electric Railway, aka "Uncle UE," which later became the United Transit Company. In 1966, it was acquired by what we know today as RIPTA.

The proliferation of automobiles and bus routes in the 1930s signaled the end of the trolley era. Service to Smithfield was discontinued in 1935, but some companies continued operations in Providence until 1948.

Some of the old trolleys were sold to other countries, and others saw new careers as diners. Those that remained were burned in a massive bonfire at Rocky Point. The only surviving trolley known to have traveled through Smithfield is displayed at the Connecticut Trolley Museum in East Windsor, Connecticut. As for the old trolley tracks, it is said by some that they still lie buried beneath the roadways of Smithfield.

CHAPTER 7

WHEN SMITHFIELD WAS "APPLE VALLEY"

Perhaps the best known agricultural product ever produced in Smithfield was apples. In fact, apple orchards were once so plentiful that Smithfield earned the nickname of "Apple Valley." Although most of the orchards have long disappeared, the name Apple Valley is still connected with no fewer than fourteen local businesses and one mall. Local street names such as Appletree Lane, Baldwin Drive, Cider Lane and numerous others also reflect the area's apple-growing heritage.

One of the most popular drinks in early America was hard cider, a fermented apple juice with a kick. Virtually everyone drank it, including children. Besides being plentiful and easy to make, it was also healthier than drinking water that in many cases was not as pure as we in the twenty-first century like to believe. Because everyone drank cider, practically every farm in New England had a few apple trees growing on it. The idea of planting trees in mass quantities for commercial purposes didn't come about until the 1860s, when westward expansion of America created a demand.

T.K. WINSOR, THE APPLE KING

Smithfield's apple industry seems to have started with James Winsor, who began growing apples for commercial use on his one-hundred-plus-acre farm in 1861. The farm, which he called Maplewood, due to the many sugar maples growing on it, was located on present-day Austin Avenue, which in the 1860s was known as Killingly Road. Today, Winsor's house is still standing but the Maplewoods housing development sits on the land where apple trees once thrived.

Winsor passed his apple business on to his son, Thomas K. Winsor, who went on to become the best-known apple grower in the state and was eventually dubbed "the Apple King" by those in the industry. Winsor built a

This is the former Thomas K. Winsor House on Austin Avenue. T.K. Winsor was said to be the undisputed "Apple King." The house was built by Captain Andrew Waterman about 1774.

business that not only sold apples locally but also shipped them throughout the United States and Europe—quite an accomplishment for a time when refrigeration was unknown.

In the 1920s, Mr. Winsor's business had grown to the point where he needed more storage space, so he made a deal to purchase the tabernacle of the famous Reverend Billy Sunday of Providence and used the lumber from the tabernacle to construct a new barn.

Another early apple grower was William Winsor, a distant relation of James Winsor, who began a commercial orchard on Pleasant View Avenue in the 1860s. He later passed the business on to his son, Nicholas Winsor, who was the president of the Greenville Bank. The home of Nicholas Winsor still stands today at 33 Pleasant View Avenue. The land behind it was developed in the 1950s, but at one time apple orchards covered the area as far back as Cedar Swamp where Willow Field is today.

Other Early Apple Growers

Also located on Pleasant View Avenue was Brown's Orchard, owned by William Brown, on land now occupied by the playing fields of the Smithfield High School. Besides apples, Mr. Brown also raised chickens and sold eggs. Longtime residents relate that huge buildings occupied by hundreds of chickens once covered part of the land.

By 1900, the Steere family of Smithfield had also established themselves as successful apple growers. The farm of Henry Steere on Mann School Road near Mapleville Road became one of the largest apple suppliers in

Rhode Island, and is still producing apples today. Orchards established by Charles, Stephen and Seth Steere were also very successful.

Several other orchards were established in Spragueville. Payette's Pleasant View Orchards, at the foot of Swan Road, was one of the first in the area. At one time, Payette's orchards covered both sides of Pleasant View Avenue from Swan Road to Tomahawk Trail. Other orchards belonging to the Jaswell, Matteo and Polseno families occupied land on Swan Road. There was also Alice Comstock's Homestead Orchards, later owned by Albert Mowry, located at Swan Road and Mann School Road.

Before the 1940s, Swan Road was an unpaved dirt road with no electricity or town water. However, in the springtime, people would come from all over just to see the apple blossoms in bloom.

Other orchards could be found on Mann School Road, such as Connor's Farm, which is now the site of an upscale housing development and walking trails. Heading west on Mann School Road from Swan Road was the farm of Peter Sasso. On Colwell Road was a farm owned by Michael Connetti. But these were not the only apple growers at that time. Besides the Winsor farm on Austin Avenue, there was also the Lockwood Farm, which is still in existence but no longer grows and sells apples, and another farm owned by a man named Herbert "Hub" Winsor. Still more orchards were located on Smith Avenue leading out of Greenville. These included Stuart Orchards and the orchard of Edwin Knight in the town of Glocester on the Smithfield line.

The farmers weren't strictly apple growers. Virtually all of them grew other types of fruit and produce, as well as kept a few cows and other animals.

The industry saw a spike during World War I, when apples were shipped overseas in wooden barrels to the troops, but the apple industry in Smithfield didn't reach its peak until the 1930s, when many farmers began growing different varieties of apples in lieu of other crops.

Although the farmers were technically in competition with one another, there was plenty of business to go around, and the apple growers helped one another in the sense of sharing advice and growing techniques. Smithfield was still a small town in those days, and anyone involved in local agriculture belonged to the Greenville Grange and the Rhode Island Fruit Growers Association. All of them took their product to the same farmers' market in Providence.

The Hurricane of 1938 toppled many of the apple trees and knocked millions of apples from their branches. Fortunately, some of the trees were young and easily righted by hand or with the help of a strong tractor. Many apples that year were too bruised for market so they were turned into cider.

In the later half of the twentieth century, many of Smithfield's apple producers went out of business, and the land was subsequently gobbled up by development. The most recent orchard to close was Matteo's Farm at 90 Swan Road, which had been in continuous operation since the 1920s.

Fortunately, there are still a few active orchards operating in Smithfield today. All are family-run businesses that have spanned generations.

Apple Orchards Still Active in Smithfield

Appleland Orchard

Appleland Orchard is owned and operated by Joseph and Louise D'Andrea. Mr. D'Andrea has been involved with growing apples for more than seventy years. His grandfather, Michael Polseno, came to Smithfield from Italy in 1890, and eventually acquired more than one hundred acres on Swan Road, where he grew many types of apples. The Polseno farm remained in operation until 1951.

D'Andrea went to work for his grandfather in 1935, when he was nine years old, and continued until he went into the army in 1945. From 1962 to

Appleland Orchard is located on the corner of Smith Avenue and West Greenville Road on the Smithfield/Glocester town line. It sells a variety of apple products, including apple wine.

1972, he ran an apple stand in Pomfret, Connecticut. In 1972, he returned to Smithfield and leased the land he presently owns from Mrs. Stewart, the widow of Harold Stewart, who had owned and operated Harold Stewart Orchards. D'Andrea ran his business as Stewart Orchards until 1973, when Mrs. Stewart sold him three acres on West Greenville Road to grow apples. At that time, he changed the name to Appleland Orchard. In 1976, he built the building that now serves as his retail store, but the original apple stand built by Mr. Stewart still exists next door.

In 1978, he bought another forty acres on Snake Hill Road in Glocester that still produce a variety of apples.

Appleland Orchards still presses its own cider on the premises and sells its own apple wine, as well as a variety of pies and preserves.

Jaswell's Farm

Jaswell's Farm can trace its origins to 1899, when Nicola Gesualdi came to Smithfield from Italy and leased some land on Swan Road. He later purchased the land and eventually acquired over one hundred acres. At some point, Nicola changed his name to Nicholas Jaswell, and the farm has been known as Jaswell's ever since.

Jaswell's Farm on Swan Road is the oldest remaining active orchard in Smithfield.

Nicholas had seven children: Peter, Charles, Joseph, Roy, Katie, Mary and Dan. One by one the children left the family farm to pursue careers other than farming. The only one to remain on the farm was Joseph, who eventually inherited the business in the early 1930s.

Joseph turned the farm over to his son Richard in 1967. Richard, along with his wife Pat, ran the farm and raised two children. In 1999, their two children, Christopher and Allison, took over the business from their parents.

Jaswell's was the first to pasteurize apple cider in Rhode Island, and still produces its own cider on the premises. Between late May and December 24, the public is invited to pick their own or visit the retail farm stand. In addition to apples, Jaswell's also sells strawberries, raspberries, blueberries and a variety of baked goods and preserves.

Hill Orchards

Hill Orchards retail outlet is located at 25 Sanderson Road near the Johnston town line, but the actual orchard is located at 86 Winsor Avenue in Johnston.

The business is presently owned by Warren and Allan Hill. It is a family business that can trace its lineage back to the 1600s, when the family farm in

Hill Orchards has this retail outlet on Sanderson Road. The actual apple orchards are located in Johnston.

Johnston was first established. However, the family didn't get into the apple business until the 1930s, when Harold and his brother Charles planted apple trees on roughly forty acres at the farm.

Harold and Charles ran the business as a wholesale orchard under the name of Hill Brothers. Charles passed away in the early 1960s and Harold continued operations. In 1974, the business began operating under the name of Hill Orchards, as it is known today.

Presently, Hill Orchards supplies fruit to local schools through wholesale buyers and participates at farmers' markets that still exist in Rhode Island. During the summer and autumn months, the farm stand offers apples, peaches, cider and pumpkins, and Christmas trees in December. The farm also offers hayrides and the ability to pick your own apples.

Steere Orchard

Steere Orchard is located at the intersection of Mapleville Road and Austin Avenue, and is presently owned and operated by Henry J. Steere Jr., who likes to go by Jim so as not to be confused with his father, Henry J. Steere Sr.

The business was started by Jim's grandfather, Arthur W. Steere, who had a farm on Steere Road off Smith Avenue in the 1800s. Arthur was quite the entrepreneur, involved with several businesses besides farming, and even served in the Rhode Island Senate in 1907. The farm began as a dairy farm, and Arthur didn't begin to grow apples until the early 1900s, when he planted about fifty acres of trees.

Steere Orchard in Greenville is still one of the largest apple growers in Rhode Island.

This barn on Colwell Road is where Donald Connetti operates his apple-processing business.

Sometime about 1930, Arthur's son, Henry J. Steere Sr., and his wife Frieda took over the orchards on Austin Avenue. The retail building used today is the same one used by Henry at that time. The building suffered some damage in the Hurricane of 1938 when heavy winds tore the roof off.

Henry Sr. passed away in 1970, and Mrs. Steere and Jim continued to operate the business. Today, the orchards consist of about three thousand apple trees and three hundred peach trees, along with a few acres of pumpkins.

In the autumn, the public is invited to pick their own apples.

Blossom Trail Orchard

Blossom Trail Orchard is no longer a working orchard, but it started out as one. It had its beginning in 1902, when Michael and Myra Connetti bought 150 acres on Colwell Road and started Connetti's Orchard. In 1906, they sold about half of their land, which is now occupied by the YMCA Camp.

Hurricane Carol of 1954 all but wiped out their business; however, after some reorganization, they reopened in 1955 as Blossom Trail Orchard, specializing in fresh sliced apples used in pies and desserts. The present owner is Donald Connetti, who continues to sell processed apples to restaurants, bakeries, hotels, schools, hospitals and nursing homes throughout New England.

CHAPTER 8

FIREFIGHTING IN SMITHFIELD

We take it for granted today that when there's a fire, we can simply pick up the phone and the fire department will respond—but such was not always the case. It is hard to imagine a time when Smithfield didn't have a fire department, and home fire protection consisted of a leather bucket kept by the door. But such a time did exist for almost 140 years.

The Smithfield Fire Department of today is a highly trained, professional organization that responds to all types of emergencies. Like many career fire departments across America, the department can trace its origins back to the days of volunteer fire companies. The volunteer companies grew out of necessity. Their earliest firefighting apparatus would seem primitive compared to the modern fire engines of today, but they were better than bucket brigades.

Throughout its history, Smithfield has had three fire companies: Greenville, Georgiaville and the lesser-known Wionkhiege Valley Volunteer Fire Company. This chapter deals with the origins of each company before they merged to become the Smithfield Fire Department as we know it today.

SMITHFIELD'S FIRST FIRE ENGINE

On the night of June 20, 1870, a terrific storm swept across the Smithfield area. Lightning flashed and thunder boomed as rain pelted the ground. About eleven o'clock, as the inhabitants of Greenville waited out the storm secure in their homes, the cry of fire went out through the village. Lightning had struck Messrs Whipple & Co.'s wheelwright shop located in the heart of Greenville.

Volunteers rushed to the scene with their buckets, but it was no use. The fire had gotten a good head start and the business was soon engulfed in flames.

The Water Witch was Smithfield's first fire engine. It disappeared during World War II and its present whereabouts are unknown. *Courtesy of the Smithfield Historical Society.*

The fire then spread to the building next door, which contained a business operated by William Tobey, and it soon became apparent that this building would also be lost. When it was over, both buildings had burned to the ground and one man had been seriously injured when he fell from a ladder.

It became apparent to the citizens of Greenville that something more in the way of fire protection was needed to prevent such an occurrence from happening again. A fundraising drive was held, and within a month, nearly $1,000 had been collected toward the purchase of a used hand-pump fire engine.

The fire engine was primitive by today's standards and obsolete even for 1870, but was a great improvement over bucket brigades. It had formerly seen service with the Dexter Hose Company in Pawtucket, where it had been dubbed "the Water Witch." It arrived in Greenville on July 4, 1870, amidst much fanfare.

The "new" fire engine needed a team of strong and hearty men to operate it. The engine had two long poles or handles running along each side. At a fire, a suction hose would be dropped into a water source such as a pond or cistern. Then several men would line up on each side of the engine and begin "pumping" by uniformly moving the handles up and down. The up stroke would draw water up into the tub portion of the engine and the down stroke would shoot the water into another hose, which would be operated by other firemen aiming it at the fire. This required teamwork as well as stamina, for it didn't take long for fatigue to set in and those on the engine would need relief.

According to a news article in the *Woonsocket Patriot*, the new fire company was dubbed "the Rescue," and the Water Witch was kept in the basement of the Smithfield Exchange Bank. Andrew B. Whipple was appointed the foreman and Martin Mann and Ethan C. Thornton were appointed first- and second-class foremen. Today these ranks are known as chief and deputy chief.

The Rescue Fire Company later became the Greenville Fire Company, which later became part of the Smithfield Fire Department as we know it today.

One enduring mystery surrounding the Water Witch is its unsolved disappearance. The engine was retired from service in 1914. Tradition runs strong in many fire departments, and the Greenville company was no exception. Rather than discard the vintage piece of equipment, it was decided to preserve it for use in parades and for special occasions.

By the late 1930s, storage of the Water Witch became a problem, so when members of the Chepachet Fire Department asked to use the engine in their town's annual Ancients and Horribles Parade, Greenville agreed, with the stipulation that they also store it for the time being.

On December 7, 1941, the United States entered World War II and the young men of both towns answered their country's call to service. After the war, Greenville firefighters went to retrieve the Water Witch, only to discover that it had disappeared and nobody seemed to know what had happened to it.

There were some who said that the antique fire engine was taken for one of the scrap metal drives during the war, but as late as 1970, a persistent rumor held that the Water Witch was being stored in a barn in Glocester. Several attempts by Greenville firemen to look in the barn were rebuffed by a caretaker. In 2006, renewed inquiries were made but without success. Perhaps one day the Water Witch will be returned to Greenville.

This Greenville fire lieutenant's badge dates to the 1950s, when Greenville and Georgiaville had two separate fire companies. Today, all badges worn by the fire department read "Smithfield Fire Department."

The Origin of the Georgiaville Fire Company

For many years, it was thought that the Georgiaville Fire Company was started in 1923. However, hand-written records now in the possession of the Smithfield Fire Department prove that the fire company actually began much earlier.

On April 20, 1915, two icehouses belonging to the Providence Ice Company burned to the ground along the shore of Georgiaville Pond with a monetary loss of $50,000. It was fires such as this that drew attention to the need for fire protection in Georgiaville.

The Georgiaville Fire Company began on April 26, 1915, when a meeting was held at Bernon Hall in Georgiaville to discuss organizing a volunteer fire company for the east side of town. Bernon Hall was owned by the Bernon Mill, the largest employer in Georgiaville. The mill owners no doubt had a vested interest in acquiring better fire protection.

A follow-up meeting was held on June 15, 1915, when a motion was carried to purchase a motorized fire truck. But the truck was never purchased. For some reason, this first attempt at organization didn't materialize, and it wasn't until two years later, on June 25, 1917, that the fire company was formally established as the Smithfield Fire Company.

The new fire company started with two pieces of hand-drawn apparatus: a hook and ladder and a chemical wagon, which were both stored at the Bernon Mill. Both apparatus were considered long obsolete for the day, but they were better than nothing.

In the autumn of 1923, the Smithfield Fire Company acquired its first motorized fire engine, a brand-new 1923 Chandler. Before long, a 1912 Packard

This photo shows the Georgiaville fire station shortly after its construction. *Courtesy of Ken Brown Sr., Smithfield Fire Department, retired.*

ladder truck and a 1912 Cadillac forest fire truck were added. Many consider 1923 to be the year the fire company was formally established as its members could now respond to fires beyond the locality of the mill in a timely fashion.

On May 27, 1924, a meeting was held at the Smithfield Town Hall (then located in the present-day VFW Post on Farnum Pike), where it was voted to abolish the Smithfield Fire Company and reestablish it as the Smithfield Volunteer Fire Department, District #2. Minutes of this meeting state that it was "voted that this company become a permanent organization."

District 2's fire engines were stored at several locations until 1924, when the old Georgiaville School was turned over to the fire department for use as a station. A total of $3,000 was raised by the company through social fundraisers to build an addition off the back of the old school to accommodate larger fire trucks.

By 1940, the fire company had outgrown its quarters and it was apparent that a new station was needed. A site was selected next to the town hall, and on October 25, 1942, the fire company relocated to what is today the Georgiaville Fire Station, aka Smithfield Fire Station #2.

The fire company continued to officially call itself the Smithfield Volunteer Fire Company, District #2, for many years, although unofficially it was called the Georgiaville Fire Company. About 1950, the name was officially changed to the Georgiaville Fire Company, and the name remained on the fire station even after Smithfield's first paid fire department was established in 1966.

THE WIONKHIEGE VALLEY VOLUNTEER FIRE COMPANY

From 1958 to 1962, there was a volunteer fire company in Smithfield that few remember today called the Wionkhiege Valley Volunteer Fire Company (WVVFC). Although it was only in existence a short time, it is still part of Smithfield's firefighting history.

During the late 1950s, the northern part of town in the area of Burlingame Road experienced an increase in development, prompting some who lived in that area to lobby for a new fire district. The idea wasn't to eliminate the need for the Greenville or Georgiaville Fire Companies, but to shorten response time and slow a fire's progress until other apparatus could arrive.

Mrs. Diane W. Latham was responsible for the organization of the new fire company, which was established in September 1958 after being granted a charter by Secretary of State John A. Notte. The Latham Farm barn, located on Log Road, was converted for use as a fire station.

At the company's first meeting, officers were elected. Daniel W. Latham was elected president; William Martineau, vice-president; Edward Jacques,

This barn on Log Road once served as the headquarters for the Wionkhiege Valley Volunteer Fire Company.

secretary; and Harry Gardner, treasurer. Mrs. Latham, Mrs. John Mura, Rutledge Mollander, Hugh Brown, Walter Goudie, Ralph Farrar and Charles Campbell were all elected to serve as a board of directors, with Mrs. Latham and Mrs. Mura also serving in the ladies' auxiliary. The signers of the charter were Daniel Latham, Edward Jacques, John Mura, Wyit Wright, John McGirr and Burton Mowry.

The new fire company held square dances to raise money for equipment and soon purchased a secondhand Ward LaFrance pumper truck from Richmond, Rhode Island. In addition to the pumper, the company also had a Ford tanker truck capable of carrying eight hundred gallons of water that the members built themselves.

The members also dug twenty strategically located water holes throughout their district to act as cisterns from which the pumper could draw in the event of a fire.

The new firemen received training from Lieutenant Ronald R. Jones of the Cranston Fire Department, as well as first aid and lifesaving courses from the Red Cross.

Surprisingly, not everyone was pleased with the formation of the new fire company, as evidenced by newspaper articles of the era. Some felt that the added fire protection wasn't needed and sought to have the company abolished. (Most likely, those who felt that way didn't live in that area of town.) In 1961, the question was put to local voters as to whether funding should be allotted to the WVVFC. Despite objections by some, voters opted to grant the funding.

For the next year the debate continued. Members of the town council requested a comprehensive study be done as to the necessity of having a

Smithfield Fire Station #3 on Log Road was built in 1964 after the Wionkhiege Valley Volunteer Fire Company was disbanded.

third fire district in the town. The study was conducted by the Smithfield Planning Board, which released a report on its findings in early 1962.The report basically stated that although a new fire district wasn't needed, there should be a fire engine stationed in the area and the engine should come under the control of the Greenville Fire Company.

Naturally, this report was not good news for the Wionkhiege firemen, who decided to fight back. They wrote a letter to the *Observer* that appeared on May 10, 1962, asking the voters of Smithfield to allow the WVVFC to continue by approving funds for it at the town financial meeting on May 12. However, despite their best efforts, the fire company was forced to disband. Afterward, the present-day Log Road fire station (Smithfield Fire Station #3) was built, which officially opened in June 1964.

THE STILLWATER MILL FIRE

One of Smithfield's most spectacular fires occurred at the historic Stillwater Mill on the morning of May 17, 1984. It was said that the smoke from the conflagration could be seen for miles, from Providence in the south to nearby Massachusetts in the north. Over two hundred firefighters battled the blaze for more than twenty-four hours, but despite their best efforts, the mill was a total loss. This is the story of what happened that day.

The Stillwater Mill was a large, imposing brick structure on Stillwater Road, at the intersection of Thurber Boulevard. It once produced textiles but at the time of the fire it was occupied by a plastics company by the name of Crystal Craft.

Howard Dunn was a security officer for Crystal Craft, and he arrived at the mill that morning about 6:25 a.m. After clocking in, he turned the

The Stillwater Mill Fire was not only spectacular, but also dangerous. Several Smithfield firefighters found themselves in a tight spot when they suddenly lost water pressure. *Courtesy of Ken Brown Sr., Smithfield Fire Department, retired.*

furnace on. Even though it was a pleasant spring morning, the furnace was needed to take the damp chill out of the building. He then went to the guard station to greet employees who began arriving for the day shift.

Shortly before 7:00 a.m., an employee discovered several cardboard boxes on fire in the warehouse portion of the building. The flames were growing rapidly, and with the sprinkler and fire alarm systems out of order for repairs, he immediately ran to alert others of the fire.

While shouts of "Fire!" rang through the complex, Officer Dunn and several others raced to the warehouse to try to fight the flames with hand-held fire extinguishers. For a brief time it appeared that the fire might be brought under control, but then someone opened a nearby garage door to let the smoke escape. This fed fresh oxygen to the flames, which sprang back with a vengeance. With the fire extinguishers exhausted, there was nothing more they could do, and the men were forced to withdraw for their own safety.

The wood of the mill was old and dry, and the floors were soaked with one hundred years of oils. The warehouse was loaded with cardboard boxes and other combustible materials. All of this added up to a perfect source of fuel for the fire, setting the stage for a major conflagration.

Nobody panicked. The building was a huge, sprawling complex with plenty of exits. The fifty workers comprising the day shift filed out in an orderly fashion while someone called the fire department. The call was received at 7:05 a.m.

Battalion Chief William J. Perry of the Smithfield Fire Department was at his home, getting ready for work, when his pager sounded, informing him of a fire at the mill. He raced to the scene and arrived before the first fire engines. He could see flames and smoke coming from the warehouse and radioed a "Code Red," indicating that it was a real fire and not a false alarm.

The fire began in the warehouse portion of the building. This is what Battalion Chief Perry of the Smithfield Fire Department saw as he arrived on the scene. *Courtesy of Ken Brown Sr., Smithfield Fire Department, retired.*

Within the next two minutes, the first two fire engines arrived. The "first in" was Engine 4, from the Log Road Station, commanded by Captain Michael R. Lusher and driven by Private William B. Ross. Chief Perry directed them to the rear of the warehouse, where thick smoke was already billowing out and flames now lit several windows. Within moments, they were joined by Tank 2 from Georgiaville, driven by Private Robert R. Peters and commanded by Lieutenant Ken Brown. Privates David B. Chartier and Michael A. LeBlanc were also aboard.

When Smithfield fire chief Walter C. Passano arrived moments later, he quickly sized up the situation and called for a "general alarm," which would bring help from several surrounding communities. By 7:15 a.m., the first alarms were ringing at fire stations in North Providence, Johnston and North Smithfield, followed by more in Scituate and Glocester.

The first two Smithfield engines carried their own water supplies. Engine 4 carried 650 gallons and Tank 2 over 1,200 gallons.

Engine 4's crew attacked the flames coming from the loading dock area while Lieutenant Brown used Tank 2's fifty-five-foot expandable boom to smash a hole through a window. At the end of the boom was a water cannon that could be pointed directly at the flames. Lieutenant Brown had set the cannon so that water would be shooting down the interior length of the warehouse in order to retard the fire's progress until more help arrived.

A short time later, Primrose Engine 4 of North Smithfield arrived and Primrose firemen connected their hoses to Tank 2 and began assisting the crew of Smithfield's Engine 4 at the loading dock.

Meanwhile, Smithfield Engine 2 had arrived and was directed to the nearest fire hydrant, which was on Thurber Boulevard. The crew members began the process of laying over 1,500 feet of hose line from the hydrant to

The two Smithfield engines at the rear of the warehouse were joined by one from Primrose. *Courtesy of Ken Brown Sr., Smithfield Fire Department, retired.*

Tank 2's location at the rear of the warehouse. Thanks to their quick work, Tank 2 was able to continue pumping once its own water supply was depleted.

Smithfield Engine 3 was directed to the north end of the warehouse, where it could draw water from the large millpond and fight the fire from there. Smithfield Engine 1 from Greenville took a position just behind Engine 3 for the same purpose. A short time later, they were joined by two out-of-town engines. One of these engines fed water to North Providence Ladder 2 positioned at the front of the mill.

In all, thirty fire engines from several communities responded to fight the fire. At the height of the blaze, more than fourteen thousand gallons of water per minute were being poured into the inferno.

The firemen at the rear of the warehouse were in a precarious situation. In addition to the heat and flames, there were also four large tanks full of highly explosive propane gas only a few feet away. Furthermore, the heat was melting the insulation off the high-voltage electrical wires overhead that carried twenty-two thousand volts of electricity. If the tanks exploded or the wires fell, it would have meant certain death or serious injury to the firefighters.

Lieutenant Brown's idea of placing the boom through the window to get at the source of the fire seemed to be working, until the hose line leading from the hydrant to Tank 2 suddenly burst. At the time this occurred, both Smithfield Engine 4 and the Primrose Engine were drawing their water from Tank 2, so when the line failed, they also lost water. The broken line was quickly repaired but then failed a second time.

With no water to stop it, the fire quickly gained headway. Before long, one window after another lit up with the light of the orange flames and then blew out from the heat. As each window fell away, fresh air fed the flames,

Lieutenant Ken Brown Sr. can be seen on the rear step of Tank 2 behind the mill. *Courtesy of Ken Brown Sr., Smithfield Fire Department, retired.*

causing the fire to move swiftly along the interior of the building and right past where Lieutenant Brown had placed the boom of Tank 2.

The process happened quickly as each window blew out in rapid succession. Flames roared out of each opening, spewing thick smoke and tremendous heat. The heat was so intense that Lieutenant Brown's air pack became fused to his fire coat. The back wall of the warehouse quickly became a massive wall of flame, causing Chief Perry to re-deploy the engines to a better position at the front of the mill.

While Lieutenant Brown retracted the boom, Smithfield Engine 4 drove past, getting its paint scorched and emergency lights melted from the heat. The Primrose engine retreated with its hose bed on fire. Tank 2 also suffered similar battle damage. The crews had to move out quickly, forcing them to abandon several hundred feet of hose line, but at least the fire trucks were saved to continue the fight. In another minute, they would have been lost.

After assessing the situation, Chief Perry regrouped the men and began a new attack from the front of the mill. Suddenly, a new danger arose when it was discovered that a nearby garage owned by a gun dealer held gunpowder and ammunition inside. The asphalt roof of the garage was already beginning to show signs of curling from the heat. Chief Perry was forced to divert resources to prevent the garage from igniting.

The fire advanced from the warehouse area into the main portion of the building. Two towers flanked the front of the mill, and soon wisps of smoke began wafting out from under the eaves, an indication that flames had spread to the attic space. The mill was now burning from top to bottom.

Before long, the roof of the first tower was in flames, and the second ignited shortly afterward. Along the front of the building, windows between the towers fell out one by one as searing heat shattered the ancient glass. As each

As each window broke away, the flames received more oxygen and grew stronger. The smoke could be seen for miles. *Courtesy of Ken Brown Sr., Smithfield Fire Department, retired.*

window surrendered itself to the fire, orange flames would spring up and leap outward, enriched by the fresh oxygen. By now it was evident that the old mill could not be saved. The fire was now so hot that streams of cold water from the fire hoses immediately turned to steam when they hit the flames. This had become a "surround and drown" operation. Firefighters now focused their attention on saving the front office portion of the mill housed in a building located in front of the structure. (Even though firefighters managed to save this portion of the mill, it was later demolished for safety reasons.)

By 9:00 a.m., just two hours after the blaze was discovered, the office portion was all that remained. It took another eleven hours to bring the fire under control, and firemen would continue to water down hot spots for another twenty-four hours.

Before the fire was out, fire officials began their investigation. Plant workers and firefighters were interviewed, and the debris was thoroughly examined for clues. Several possibilities as to the cause were considered, but nothing could be conclusively proven. In the end, the cause of the fire could not be determined and the case was closed.

Two months later, Chief Passano presented Chief Perry and the Smithfield fire crews of Engine 4 and Tank 2 with commendations for their calmness in the face of danger.

The Stillwater Mill site dated back to 1824, when two brothers, Israel and Welcome Arnold, built a small cotton mill there. The mill changed hands twice and suffered several fires where it was burned and rebuilt over the years.

In 1867, a man named Edward W. Brown established the Stillwater Woolen Mill Company on the site. The five-story brick mill measured 130 by 52 feet, with two ells 40 by 65 feet and 45 by 32 feet. It was powered by a 22-foot waterfall moving a wheel that generated about one hundred horsepower.

By 9:00 a.m., less than two hours after the fire began, the mill was a total loss. *Courtesy of Ken Brown Sr., Smithfield Fire Department, retired.*

The mill employed about 175 people and manufactured 600,000 pounds of wool a year. That mill was also destroyed by fire and rebuilt in 1871.

About 1914, the mill was purchased by the Lister family and converted to making textiles. In 1974, it was bought by a man who then sold it to Crystal Craft in 1978. In 1983, Crystal Craft sold it to Stillwater Pond Associates, which then sold it on April 30, 1984, to Balvor Associates.

After the fire, the rubble of the old mill was hauled away. Since that time, the site has sat vacant and is now overgrown with trees and brush. Every mill that occupied that site was destroyed by fire. Should a new building ever be constructed there, it is hoped that history will not repeat itself.

In Memoriam

Firefighting is inherently dangerous, and throughout its history, the town of Smithfield has lost four firefighters in the line of duty.

The first was Raymond W. Segee, who was stricken while responding to an alarm at the Greenville fire station in October 1956. He died October 7 at Roger Williams Hospital.

The next was Robert D. Brown, who suffered fatal injuries on April 2, 1960, when he fell from a moving fire truck on Farnum Pike while responding to a brush fire.

Lieutenant Eugene E. Dorgan died when he too fell from a moving fire truck while responding to what turned out to be an arson fire on September 6, 1964.

Leo Kennedy Sr. suffered a fatal heart attack during a training exercise on October 29, 1979.

These men are mentioned here so their sacrifice to the town will not be forgotten.

Chapter 9
Law Enforcement in Smithfield

The Smithfield Police Department is one of the finest and best-equipped police departments in the state. The officers not only receive the best training available, but they also have tools at their disposal that would have seemed like science fiction fifty years ago. Powerful, comfortable patrol cars with onboard computers that can run criminal checks in a matter of seconds are but one example. A rookie officer today probably can't imagine a time when computers weren't a part of everyday police work, or a time when there was no police academy and training consisted of what a senior officer thought important enough to mention. The rest you learned as you went along. But such a time did exist, not only in Smithfield but in every city and town.

The Days of Town Sergeants and Constables

Technically, law enforcement in Smithfield had its beginning when Smithfield was still part of Providence. It was in 1663, twenty-seven years after Roger Williams settled Rhode Island, that the office of high sheriff of Providence County was established. The high sheriff was a powerful position, and the sheriff appointed deputies as he saw fit to enforce the laws of Providence County.

For more than 250 years, Providence County sheriff's deputies could be found in many rural communities working closely with local constables and town sergeants until municipalities began to establish permanent police departments. Many departments began with elected or appointed town sergeants. Besides his other duties, the town sergeant served as the chief law enforcement officer who oversaw the constables. The constabulary system was based on that used in England at the time.

At Smithfield's first town meeting, held March 17, 1730, Uriah Mowry was chosen as Smithfield's first town sergeant. David Comstock, Elisha Steere and Joseph Herendeen Jr. were appointed as constables. These men were for all intents Smithfield's first police officers, although the word "police" didn't come into use until much later.

Town records show that in 1738 a pair of stocks and a whipping post were erected near the home of John Sayles in present-day Lincoln. The world was a different place in colonial America, especially before the Constitution and the Bill of Rights came into being. Convicted criminals could be made to stand in the stocks for long periods of time, endure whippings, have their ears cropped, be branded with hot irons and even put to death for acts that would seem minor today.

When the town was divided in 1871, Smithfield became as we know it today. Each of the new towns appointed its own town sergeants and constables.

One might think that there was little need for lawmen in the early days of Smithfield, but such was not the case. Theft of livestock was a problem. Travelers on rural back roads were sometimes robbed by highwaymen, and other crimes of violence occurred.

In November 1872, a Georgiaville man came home drunk and began beating his wife. The husband was shot and killed by a neighbor when the wife ran to his home for assistance.

On August 30, 1873, a Greenville woman was shot and killed when she broke down the door to a neighbor's apartment with an axe, believing her husband to be inside with another woman.

There were also the "routine" petty crimes to deal with. In December 1884, a Georgiaville woman was arrested for stealing clothing from a boardinghouse.

Law enforcement in Smithfield continued under the constabulary system into the Twentieth Century. However, as the 1900s progressed, it became obvious that something more was needed.

On the evening of January 3, 1908, a young woman was murdered for her paycheck as she walked home from her job at a Greenville mill. The investigation fell to Smithfield's town sergeant, Jenkes Smith, who wisely contacted the Providence Police for assistance. Inspector John T. Haran was sent to lend his expertise. This practice of using big-city detectives in such investigations was not unusual in rural America in those days. The killer was arrested a few days later.

The Smithfield town sergeant was appointed by the town council each November. Constables were also appointed at that time, usually from a list

This brass, hand-stamped badge is the earliest known Smithfield police badge still in existence. It was worn by Sayles Williams (1845–1927). *Historical Society of Smithfield Collection.*

of names submitted to the council by the town sergeant. The town sergeant could also appoint special constables for brief periods of time when deemed necessary. For example, at a town meeting held June 1, 1914, the town sergeant was authorized to appoint special constables for the July Fourth weekend, and each constable would be paid five dollars.

There were also some constables who carried special titles, such as "Special Constable for the Prosecution of Tramps." Apparently hobos were a problem in the days when railroads ran through Smithfield. There was also a "Special Constable to Enforce Bird Law." It is assumed that this had to do with poultry regulations. Each of these special constables was paid fifty dollars a year for his services.

Apparently the town sergeant and his constables did not attend to regular patrol duties like police officers of today, at least not at first. In the days before World War I, there were no assigned beats to patrol. Instead, it seems the police operated on a more or less "call us if you need us" basis. However, times were changing. In 1913, more trolley lines were brought into Smithfield, carrying with them outsiders. In April 1914, two stores were burglarized in Georgiaville, prompting the town council to offer a $100 reward for the person or persons responsible.

At a town meeting held June 25, 1914, a citizen's petition was submitted to the town council requesting a constable to be assigned exclusively to patrol in Esmond. The petition was accepted and then tabled, but the matter continued to be brought up over the next few months until it was finally voted on June 16, 1915, to authorize two constables for patrol duty, one for Esmond and the other for Georgiaville. The constables were only required to patrol on alternate weekends, for which they received an annual salary of $100. Jenckes Smith was authorized to patrol Greenville on weekends for the sum of $200 a year. This was the beginning of regular patrol areas in the town of Smithfield.

It was at the same June town meeting that Jenckes Smith, Charles Lakey and George Thurber were appointed as a committee to come up with a set of rules and regulations to govern the police constables. This was the first step toward the formal organization of the police department.

It was also in 1915 that the town council had a telephone installed in the town sergeant's home at taxpayer expense.

There was no police station in those days, and any prisoners had to be lodged at one of two bridewells operated by the town or at the Providence County Jail, for which the town would receive a bill from the jailer for services rendered. A bridewell is an old English term meaning house of correction, or jail. The town kept two bridewells, one in Greenville and the other in Georgiaville. Town records dated 1917 indicate that Jenckes Smith was keeper of the Greenville bridewell and Constable Joseph F. Sargent was keeper of the bridewell in Georgiaville. It is recorded that each man received fifty dollars per year for his services. Just how long the bridewells remained in operation is unclear, but it is known that they were in use as early as 1909 and as late as 1937.

In 1917, Georgiaville and Esmond each received an additional constable for weekend patrols, bringing the total number to four. Each officer received five dollars per weekend.

Town council minutes of March 9, 1918, refer to Jenckes Smith as "Chief of Police" for the first time, although he was still referred to at other times as "Town Sergeant" in later entries.

The first record of Smithfield police officers wearing uniforms is found in the town meeting records for June 14, 1919, when Chief Smith was authorized to purchase eight uniform coats and hats at a cost not to exceed $200. Seven officers besides himself were specifically named to be the recipients of said uniforms. Apparently, other officers had to buy their own if they wanted one. The first uniforms were dark blue, which was customary for the time. The gray uniforms that Smithfield officers wear today were first introduced in the autumn of 1978.

All police constables were issued a badge and a nightstick by the town clerk. However, there were apparently some who neglected to return these items upon termination of service. To rectify this, on January 10, 1920, the town council passed a requirement that each new officer pay a two-dollar deposit upon receipt of the items, which was to be given back when the items were returned.

In November 1920, Chief Smith applied to the town council for permission to buy overcoats for his officers. The request was tabled.

There is a humorous notation in the town council minutes dated November 8, 1920, which indicates that complaints of speeding automobiles had been received, but apparently the matter did not seem to be a cause of great concern, for the notation reads: "Voted that the chief of police take up the matter of auto speeders as soon as is convenient to him."

In April 1921, it was decided to end the weekend patrols in Esmond and Georgiaville, with no reason given. The department's six paid regular officers were voted pay raises to seventy-five dollars per year.

On June 11, 1921, Chief Smith was directed by the town council to stop the "peddling of ice cream" within town limits from vehicles on Sundays. The following month he was ordered to remove all gambling devices from the town. That September he was allocated funds to paint traffic directional arrows on paved roads to aid motorists. In May 1922, he was ordered to enforce the Volstead Act, which ushered in the Prohibition era.

In 1922, the Smithfield Police Department consisted of one chief, six regular paid officers and twenty-six constables. This was still primarily a part-time agency. There was no union, and an officer could be removed for minor infractions, either real or perceived. Town records show that while some officers remained on the department for many years, others had relatively short tenure. Occasionally, one or two officers would be appointed in the middle of the year instead of in November. There were no written tests to become a police officer, and no standard of physical fitness or educational requirements. All of that would come later.

The Rhode Island State Police was established in 1925 and opened a barracks in the Major William Smith House located on Waterman Avenue at the bottom of Esmond Street. One resident recalled how, as a young teenager in the 1940s, he and his friends would search for night crawlers (worms used for fishing) on the property using kerosene lamps because the grass was watered regularly. The troopers would usually come out and assist the kids by using their powerful five-cell flashlights.

Before the days of police cars, officers patrolled on horseback, bicycle or on foot.

Town records show that a motorcycle was purchased for the police department in April 1923 with the intent to "control auto traffic." Officer Robert E. Tobin was designated as the town's first motor patrol officer, and was paid one dollar an hour to enforce the motor vehicle laws. As a "traffic cop," it was also his responsibility to purchase and maintain a traffic control device known as a "silent policeman" that was installed at a location

The Major William Smith House on Waterman Avenue was built in 1703. In the 1930s, it served as a state police barracks.

known as "Sullivan's Corner." (Exactly where this location was has been lost to history.) The silent policeman was a traffic control device made of metal or concrete, usually with a light at the top, to route automobiles safely through an intersection. Town records show that Smithfield obtained its silent policeman from North Providence at a cost of $8.80.

In 1930, Smithfield obtained its first police car, a Ford Model A roadster, complete with convertible top and rumble seat.

In 1931–32, William Kelley became Smithfield's new chief of police. He also served as the town sergeant. By this time, both jobs were distinctly different and were listed as two separate offices for the town. Chief Kelley served until 1935, when he was replaced by Alfred N. Lacroix.

THE FIRST ATTEMPTS AT FORMAL ORGANIZATION

In May 1937, the town council passed a police ordinance that was recorded in Record Book 9, on page 18. Portions of the ordinance are summarized below:

- The town council would appoint the chief of police, the deputy chief and all police constables.
- The chief and deputy chief would remain employed at the pleasure of the town council. The chief's duty hours were set from 10:00 a.m. to 3:00 p.m., six days a week, with his one day off determined by the town council. The deputy chief worked the same hours and worked the chief's day off. Both were always subject to call even if off duty.
- Constables would be required to give $2.50 to the town clerk as a deposit for their badge. The badge number would be recorded by the town

clerk. However, when the officer returned the badge at the end of his term, he would only receive $0.50 back. This portion did not apply to "regularly employed members of the police department."

- To be a police officer, an applicant had to be able to read and write the English language, and be a qualified voter in the town.
- It was required that the police department keep and maintain a record book of all complaints, accidents, arrests, the names of those involved and any other work performed by on-duty officers.
- Each officer was also required to keep a log book of his activities, including dates and hours worked, and the amount of time spent on investigations.
- Officers were expected to conduct themselves in a manner that would not bring discredit to the department. They were forbidden to use profanity, drink liquor or frequent places that sold liquor, unless it was in the performance of their duty.

The ordinance specifically stated that Alfred N. Lacroix be appointed Smithfield's first full-time chief of police on June 1, 1937, even though he had been serving in the position since 1935. His salary was set at $1,450 a year. Napoleon B. Girard was appointed deputy chief at a salary of $200 a year. Paid patrolmen received $75 per year.

This ordinance was the first of its kind for the Smithfield police, and basically set on paper what had been common practice anyway.

In 1937, the police department traded in its Model A Ford for a used 1935 Ford sedan, which was better suited for police work. Bids were also taken at that time to install a police radio. The radio was one way, meaning it could receive calls but could not transmit an acknowledgement.

In 1939, Julius Boulia was appointed chief of police at an annual salary of $1,488.99. The position of deputy chief was eliminated and the paid department now consisted of four men. During World War II, Alfred Lacroix was reappointed to the chief's job until he was replaced in 1945 by Joseph P. Colura Jr.

After World War II, there were some who realized that the town had grown to the point where a full-time police department was warranted, but others disagreed and felt that things should remain as they were. Political infighting over the issue pushed the topic into the newspapers.

In 1946, the town council approved three full-time positions for the department: a chief and two sergeants. The first sergeants were Helric E. Pechie and Charles E. Campbell. The department was still supplemented by a team of police constables, or "reserves," as they came to be called. However, two years later, a new town council wanted to go back to a part-time police department. A compromise was reached in which the town council appointed its own chief and sergeants.

The reasons for opposing a permanent police department were based in politics. Some cited the fact that there were other towns similar to Smithfield that had no permanent police force, and felt that the elected town council should continue to control who was appointed to the police department. Others criticized that there was no stability under this system and complained that the department was subject to political control. The question was hotly debated until the Rhode Island General Assembly finally passed an act creating a full-time police department for Smithfield in 1950.

A PERMANENT FORCE IS ESTABLISHED

In 1950, the police department consisted of Chief Arthur B. Gould, Deputy Chief Adolph E. Schenck and Sergeant Benjamin Crossman, who commanded a cadre of nine part-time police officers and thirty-five reserve officers. This was the beginning of Smithfield's permanent police department as we know it today. Chief Gould remained in charge of the department for many years afterward.

In the 1950s, Smithfield's full-time police officers worked nine-hour days, six days a week, for roughly forty-two dollars a week. There was no additional pay for working overtime or for appearing in court. There was no medical plan, paid sick days, pension plan or uniform allowance.

New officers were issued a badge, a whistle, handcuffs and a six-shot .38-caliber revolver, which was the standard issue sidearm of virtually all police departments of that time. If an officer needed a new uniform shirt or trousers, he had to appear before the Smithfield Police Association, which was made up of members of the department, to make a formal request. The association raised funds for buying uniforms and equipment by holding an annual policeman's ball.

The police station consisted of three rooms at the town hall. The holding cell was in the basement, and the bars of this cell were only removed a few years ago. Today this area is used for storage.

Often there would only be one officer on duty for the entire town. If the officer was out of the police station, he would leave a sign in the window advising anyone who needed the police to call the department's telephone number. The station had one phone line that carried an extension to the chief's home. When the extension rang, whoever answered it would take down the information. If the call was important, the message would be relayed to the state police in Scituate, which in turn would broadcast it to the patrol officer via radio. Smithfield had only one police car at that time, and the radio was set to the state police frequency of 42.62 Megahertz. This was not the most reliable system, as many police car radios of that era could receive messages but not transmit them. They were also subject to weather interference and so-called "dead zones" where the signal could not be received. Portable police radios like the ones carried by today's officers on their duty belts did not exist, and if the officer was away from the car he would miss the broadcast. It wasn't until 1953 that the department got a second patrol car and a two-way radio system. A two-way radio was also installed in the chief's home to eliminate the need to call the state police.

By the 1960s, the department provided steady, around-the-clock coverage for the town with twenty-four-hour manning of the police station. It was during this time frame that the department received a teletype machine, a forerunner to the National Crime Information Computer. The teletype resembled a typewriter with a large spool of paper "tape" on one side. An officer would type out a message on a keyboard that would punch holes in the paper tape. A typical message might be to alert surrounding jurisdictions to watch for a stolen car and then give its description. The portion of the paper bearing the message would then be fed into the machine and the machine would "read" the punched holes and transmit the message via phone lines. One major drawback was that if the officer made a typing mistake, the whole message had to be done over. A teletype machine will only be found in a museum today, but in the 1950s and '60s they revolutionized police communications.

On December 10, 1968, Patrolman Norman Vezina died in the line of duty while attempting to rescue a five-year-old boy who had fallen through the ice on the Lower Spragueville Reservoir. Both he and the boy drowned before help could reach them. That night, at a special town council meeting, Patrolman Vezina was posthumously promoted to the rank of sergeant. The thirty-eight-year-old officer had served as a reserve police officer with the department for eighteen months before being sworn in as a permanent officer on May 1, 1968.

In 1969, the Rhode Island Municipal Police Training Academy was established, which set the professional standards of training for all Rhode Island police officers. Before this, training of police officers was left to individual departments, and the amount of training officers received varied from one jurisdiction to another.

As a side note to law enforcement history in Smithfield, some may be surprised to learn that in 1971, the United States Marshal's Service established a "safe house" in the sleepy village of Stillwater, where some of New England's most notorious criminals were housed as "guests" of Uncle Sam until they could testify in court before being put into the Witness Protection Program. Unfortunately for the marshals, the safe house quickly

This former mill owner's home on Stillwater Road once served as a "safe house" for some of New England's most notorious criminals.

became an "open secret" and was shut down in 1973 when news crews began filming activities there. Today, the house is a private residence.

A NEW POLICE STATION

During the 1960s, the department outgrew its quarters at the town hall, but taxpayers were reluctant to approve funding for a new police station. It wasn't until May 1971 that voters finally approved $150,000 for a new station, but only by a thin margin.

A building committee was appointed shortly afterward and had its first meeting on June 29, 1971. It was about this time that two Smithfield residents, Burton and Mary Mowry, came forward with the offer to donate a parcel of land they owned on Pleasant View Avenue for the new station. The offer was readily accepted and the present police station sits on this land, which is almost in the geographical center of the town.

The original building was going to be a bare bones, no frills, plain steel structure, but thanks to the efforts of Hugh J. McVay, William J. Lynch and Senator Claiborne Pell, a grant of $237,600 was obtained from the Economic Development Commission. The grant allowed for the much nicer station that the department has today.

To help defray expenses, members of the department donated their time to work on site preparation and interior construction. Construction began on May 27, 1972, and the station was officially occupied on November 18 of that year. The final cost of the project was $387,600. The interior of the building has been remodeled several times over the years but the exterior is essentially the same.

THE MODERN ERA

Smithfield police uniforms of the 1960s and early '70s consisted of dark blue trousers and light blue shirts. The uniform hat was a Stetson of the type worn by the Rhode Island State Police.

In 1973, the uniform badge and shoulder patch were redesigned to include an image of the new police station. In 1978, the department changed to the charcoal gray uniforms and patrol cars still in use today. It was also about this time that the department upgraded from the traditional .38 "police special" to Smith & Wesson, stainless steel, .357-magnum revolvers.

The police department continued to have part-time, or reserve, police officers into the 1980s. Reserve officers went through a mini academy run by the department and, upon completion, had the same police powers as any full-time officer. The reserves supplemented the regular force by working special details and functions, as well as filling patrol vacancies created when regular officers were sick or on vacation. The uniforms worn by the reserves were identical to those worn by members of the regular department, with the exception of the badge. While regular officers wore the new, colorful enameled badges, the reserves wore the plainer, old-style badges worn since 1950.

Many Rhode Island police departments had reserve officers to supplement their regular force at that time. Unfortunately, by the early 1990s, changing times and issues of liability forced virtually all police departments, Smithfield being one of them, to disband their reserve forces.

In November 1990, retired deputy chief of police James H. McVey wrote a concise history of the Smithfield Police Department beginning in the late 1940s. It can be viewed on the Smithfield Police website at www.

This badge and uniform patch were worn by Smithfield police officers from the 1950s until 1973.

This badge and patch style have been worn since 1973. The first badges, issued in 1973, carried the title of patrolman with a number at the bottom. Current badges have the generic title of officer, with "R.I." at the bottom.

smithfieldpd.com. Some of the information contained in this chapter comes from his research.

During the late 1990s, the department computerized all of its record keeping and operational systems, which included the installation of computers in the patrol cars.

In March 2001, the department became nationally accredited by the Commission on Accreditation for Law Enforcement Agencies, which means that the department met or exceeded certain professional standards as set forth by the commission.

Police work in the new century emphasized community policing. In answer to this, a police substation was opened at the Apple Valley Mall. It remained in operation for a few years before it was moved to Smithfield Crossings.

In 2003, the department purchased its first boat, an eighteen-foot aluminum boat powered by a sixty-horsepower motor for use on various lakes and ponds.

In January 2005, the Smithfield, Glocester, North Smithfield and Burrillville Police Departments together purchased a thirty-eight-foot mobile command center with Homeland Security funds. The vehicle is designed to be a self-sufficient mobile command post capable of responding to disaster situations in northwest Rhode Island.

In April 2008, the department received its first police canine, a German Shepherd named Paxson, and Officer Mike Gilmore became the department's first K-9 officer.

The Smithfield Police Department has come a long way since its humble beginnings. Today there are forty-one sworn officers. One can only surmise that the department will continue to grow as time goes on.

Chapter 10

Smithfield's Aviation History

The Wright brothers first flew at Kitty Hawk, North Carolina, in 1903, thus proving that mechanical flight of airplanes was possible. This ushered in the era of modern aviation. It is unknown when the first airplane came to Smithfield, but the town has seen its share of aviation-related events. Among them are a man who invented perhaps the world's first aircraft service and repair station; the creation of two airports; numerous aircraft accidents; and a visit from a young pilot who played a role in World War II history.

Arthur C. Gould

In September 1926, Smithfield resident Arthur C. Gould came up with a novel idea and established "Flyer's Haven" at his farm on Ridge Road—the first and, as far as it is known, only "aircraft service and repair station" in the state. Gould wanted to give pilots a place where they could land to refuel or receive any needed repairs much like an automobile would drive into a service station on a highway. Gould carried the special high-octane gasoline needed by most aircraft, and his farm was equipped with a wood shop, a blacksmith shop and a four-hundred-foot pond that could accommodate sea planes. To guide the way to his business, Gould used white lime to make huge arrows and letters on the ground that could be seen from the air. Since airplane engines of that era were about as reliable as car engines, Gould no doubt expected to see a lot of business, but for some reason, the idea never really caught on.

SMITHFIELD AIRPORTS

Today, everyone is familiar with North Central Airport, located in the northeast portion of town, but not many are aware that Smithfield once had an earlier airport that was located where Bryant University stands today.

The birth of Smithfield's first airport came about when John F. Emin Sr., a farm owner on John Mowry Road, bought a Curtis, Pusher airplane in July 1931. He kept the plane at What Cheer Airport in Pawtucket but wanted a place that was more convenient. In early 1932, while on a visit to New Bedford, he saw an airplane hangar for sale. He bought it, had it disassembled and brought it to his farm in Smithfield. There he reassembled it, and after clearing a cornfield for an airstrip, Smithfield had its first airport, aptly named the Smithfield Airport.

The airport was nothing more than a hangar and a grass field for landings and takeoffs. There was no control tower, landing lights or tarmac, and the only weather technology available for arriving planes was a brightly colored windsock, yet the airport quickly proved to be very popular with aviation enthusiasts and locals alike.

When Emin built his airport, he unwittingly set the stage for an event that would play a minor part in World War II history. On December 22, 1934, a young army lieutenant of the Pennsylvania (Air) National Guard needed to make an emergency landing during a raging snowstorm. Ice had been building on his plane's wings and the aircraft was in danger of crashing. By chance, he suddenly saw the Smithfield Airport below and managed to land safely despite the drifting snow.

Once on the ground, he was met by Emin, who offered the use of his personal car so the lieutenant could drive to a store in Stillwater that had a phone and

This photo shows John F. Emin's (Sr.) Curtis Pusher airplane, which he bought in 1931. It was his love of flying that led to the creation of Smithfield's first airport. *Courtesy of John F. Emin Jr.*

report to his superiors that he had not crashed in the storm. Afterward, the lieutenant was allowed to stay at the Emin house until the weather cleared. The lieutenant never forgot the kindness bestowed upon him, and over the years that followed, he kept up a pen pal relationship with the Emins.

The lieutenant's name was William G. Benn, who later enlisted in the U.S. Army Air Corps at the beginning of World War II and went on to serve as part of General Kenny's staff in the Pacific. At that time, the Allies were having a difficult time using high-altitude bombers to sink enemy ships that were resupplying Japanese strongholds. In response to this, Major Benn, as he was then known, developed a new bombing technique known as "skip bombing," which allowed Allied bombers to sink enemy ships by skipping a bomb across the water like one would skip a stone. The new technique proved highly successful and no doubt saved many American lives and helped to shorten the war.

For his work, Major Benn received the Distinguished Service Cross, and was even written about in the January 18, 1943 issue of *Time* magazine. Unfortunately, Major Benn did not survive the war. He was lost on a mission the same day the magazine hit the newsstands. Had John Emin's airport not been in existence, it could be argued that Major Benn might not have lived to develop his skip bombing technique. Thus, the old Smithfield Airport can hold its place as a footnote to history.

In the 1940s, the Smithfield Airport was considered as a potential site for a second state airport that would be comparable with T.F. Greene, but it never came to pass. Instead, the state opted to build North Central Airport.

The Smithfield Airport continued operating until the mid-1950s. The property was eventually sold to Earl S. Tupper of Tupperware fame, who later gave it to Bryant College (now Bryant University). Bryant developed the site for a new college campus, which opened in 1971. When the campus initially opened, the old Smithfield Airport hangar was used by the maintenance department until it was torn down about 1980 and replaced by a larger building.

North Central Airport gets its name for being located in the northern-central portion of the state. One reason that it wasn't named the Smithfield Airport was because that name was already taken. Planning for North Central Airport began in March 1945, when members of the Woonsocket and Pawtucket Chambers of Commerce met to discuss the feasibility of creating an airport that could service the Blackstone Valley region at the close of World War II. Four months later, the present-day site of North Central Airport was chosen, and the Providence Chamber of Commerce weighed in with its support for the project.

The main terminal at North Central Airport has changed very little since it was built in 1950–51.

In early 1946, questionnaires were mailed to residents who would be affected by the airport to see what they thought of the project. The results of these questionnaires were not recorded, but it can be surmised that public reaction was similar to what it would be today if such a proposal was made.

Despite any protests, by late 1946, 862 acres of land were condemned by the state for the project. However, due to political infighting, rising cost estimates and problems with funding, actual clearing of the land didn't begin until February 1950. Construction took another twenty-two months, and the official dedication didn't take place until December 15, 1951. Although initial construction estimates in 1945 set the cost of building the airport at $50,000, the total cost was $1.4 million.

The dedication ceremonies had to be scaled down due to weather, but that didn't stop a New England Helicopter Service helicopter from carrying 1,700 pieces of mail out of the airport to the Saylesville Post Office in Lincoln. The mail contained souvenir cachets that received a special stamp before being mailed out. Today, these cachets are highly sought after by collectors.

North Central Airport was designed with the potential for expansion in mind; however, until fairly recently, very little expansion has taken place since the 1950s. The airport is one of five "satellite" airports in the state that cater to general aviation aircraft. Planes land and take off at their own risk, as the control tower is unmanned.

In 2008, the wooded areas surrounding the airport were cut down and cleared under the direction of the Department of Homeland Security. It was during this process that a "lost" historical cemetery was discovered. The cemetery was last recorded in a 1919 survey, but modern attempts to locate it had been unsuccessful. The Smithfield Historical Cemetery Commission has since marked and recorded the cemetery.

Aviation Accidents

The first known aviation accident to occur in Smithfield happened on September 14, 1930, when a biplane carrying two brothers crashed into a tree just off Austin Avenue near River Road. The brothers, Walter and Robert Barnes, walked away with only minor injuries.

Unfortunately, six months later, on March 15, 1931, they were involved in another plane crash that severely injured Robert and took the life of Walter. On that morning, they became lost in heavy fog over Greenville, and crashed into a hillside on the farm of Lloyd E. Dodge off Tarklin Road.

There have been dozens of aviation accidents documented to have happened in Smithfield since 1960, when official records began to be kept, and probably just as many occurred before reporting was required.

One longtime resident who grew up near the Smithfield Airport stated that he had witnessed "four or five" crashes in his youth, none of which was serious in the sense of injuries, yet they were totally destructive to the aircraft. Since there were no requirements to file a report, the wrecks were simply hauled off the field with a tractor. Local kids would play on them until the owner either came to retrieve his plane or it was taken away as junk.

The only known fatal crash to occur at the Smithfield Airport happened on May 28, 1934, when a plane crashed shortly after takeoff, killing two men.

On August 25, 1940, a young man demolished his airplane in an apple orchard next to the airport, yet he walked away unharmed. Undeterred by this experience, he flew in another plane just twenty minutes later.

Perhaps the most famous crash to occur in Smithfield was the U.S. Army, twin-engine, RB-34 that went down on Wolf Hill on August 5, 1943, killing all three servicemen aboard. Due to wartime secrecy, rumor and speculation as to the "real" reason for the accident led to stories that persisted for many years. However, the truth is that the plane was on a ferry mission from one airfield to another when it developed engine trouble and crashed.

The dead were Lieutenant Otis R. Portweig, the pilot; Sergeant Herbert D. Booth, the crew chief; and Lieutenant Saul Winsten, a passenger. These men are the only three servicemen to die in the performance of their duty during wartime within the boundaries of Smithfield. The crash occurred at latitude 41.892222 and longitude 71.528972. (For a more detailed account of this tragedy, including witness statements, look on the Smithfield town website under "history.")

Other notable accidents include a crash that occurred on the Nadeau Farm off Lime Rock Road on August 19, 1970, in which one man was killed. Seven years later, on February 4, 1977, two men were killed in another crash on the same farm.

On June 28, 1978, a man was struck and killed by a spinning propeller at North Central Airport.

On October 29, 1978, a hot air balloon made an unexpected landing on Stillwater Road. There were no injuries.

On May 23, 1979, an aircraft made an emergency landing in the field that once existed next to Route 295 where the Smithfield Crossings Mall is located today.

On April 21, 1986, a pilot was killed when his plane crashed and exploded in the woods as he was attempting to land at North Central Airport.

Two people died in a crash off Mann School Road on November 7, 1988. Two years later, on March 8, 1990, two men were killed in the same general area when their plane crashed in the woods on the Judson Farm off Williams Road.

The worst aviation accident to occur in Smithfield in terms of loss of life happened on September 8, 1997, when five people were killed when the small plane they were in crashed on takeoff.

As of this writing, the most recent accident happened on November 17, 2008, in which two men were killed when their plane crashed about one thousand feet off Clark Road.

This list is by no means complete and only accounts for some of the more notable accidents that have occurred within Smithfield. It does not account for aircraft that took off from North Central Airport but crashed in nearby Lincoln.

Epilogue

Smithfield's Time Capsule

It seems only fitting to end this book with a story that looks toward the future. Some may have already forgotten that in December 2000, the Smithfield 2000 Celebration Committee buried a time capsule near the senior center in Deerfield Park to be opened in 2050. It is my hope that by writing this, the time capsule and its location will not be forgotten, as has happened in other communities with other time capsules. After all, a lot can happen in fifty years. Buildings can be expanded, markers moved and time capsules lost or forgotten. Therefore, this is to remind Smithfield residents of the future that there is a time capsule waiting to be opened.

A notice appeared in a local newspaper in early 2000 announcing that people were welcome to submit their suggestions as to what should go into the time capsule. The items were to represent what Smithfield and our culture was like in the year 2000. The capsule was buried in December 2000—nine months before September 11, 2001, when the world and our culture were changed forever. And what items does it contain? That remains to be seen. But when it's finally opened, those items will no doubt reflect a simpler time.

In the year AD 2000, a time capsule was buried next to the flagpole at the Smithfield Senior Center in Deerfield Park. It is supposed to be opened in 2050. How much will this view have changed when it is opened?

BIBLIOGRAPHY

Town Records

Town of Smithfield, Rhode Island, Death Records, 1871 to present.

Town of Smithfield, Rhode Island, Tax Books.

Town of Smithfield, Rhode Island, Town Council Minutes Records, 1871 to present.

Maps

D.G. Beers & Co. Atlas. 1870 map of Smithfield.

Everts & Richards, 1895 map of Smithfield. Providence County, RI: New Topographical Atlas of Surveys, 1895.

Matteson, George E. 1947 map of Smithfield.

Whaling, A.F. 1851 map of Providence County.

———. 1855 map of Providence County.

Books

Bayles, Richard M. *History of Providence County R.I.* W.W. Preston & Co., 1891.

Bicknell, Tom William. *History of Rhode Island and Providence Plantations*. 1920.

Church, Colonel Benjamin. *Diary of King Philip's War 1675–1676*. Pequot Press, 1975.

Greene, Welcome Arnold. *The Providence Plantation for 250 Years*. J.A. & R.A. Reid Publishers, 1886.

Karr, Ronald Dale. *Lost Railroads of New England.* 2ed Edition. Pepperell, MA: Branch Line Press, 1996, 1989.

———. *The Rail Lines of Southern New England: A Handbook of Railroad History.* Pepperell, MA: Branch Line Press, 1995.

Leach, Douglas Edward. *Flintlock and Tomahawk.* New York: MacMillian, 1958.

Mavor, James W., Jr., and Byron E. Dix. *Manitou.* Rochester, VT: Inner Traditions International, Ltd., 1989.

Nebiker, Walter A. *Historical and Architectural Resources of Smithfield, Rhode Island: Rhode Island Historical Preservation Commission.* Rhode Island State Historical Preservation Commission, 1992.

———. *The History of North Smithfield.* Somersworth, NH: New England History Press, 1976.

Raymo, Chet, and Maureen E. Raymo. *Written in Stone: A Geological History of the Northeastern United States.* Hensonville, NY: Black Dome Press, 1989.

Steere, Thomas. *History of the Town of Smithfield from Its Organization, in 1730–1, To Its Division, In 1871.* E.L. Freeman & Co., 1881.

Swanberg, J.W. *New Haven Power 1838–1868.* N.p.: Alvin F. Staufer Publishers, 1988.

Tougas, Michael, and Eric Schultz. *King Philip's War.* Woodstock, VT: Countryman Press, 1999.

Trento, Salvatore Michael. *The Search for Lost America: The Mysteries of the Stone Ruins.* Chicago: Contemporary Books Inc., 1978.

JOURNALS

NEARA Journal

OTHER SOURCES

Architectural illustration of Stillwater Mill Complex, January 1914.

Barmann, Timothy C. "Cessna 182 Aircraft Has Good Safety Record." *Providence Journal*, September 8, 1997.

Benn, William. "Dropping in on Old New England." *Pennsylvania Guardsman* 38, no. 3 (March 1935): 10.

Bruno, James V. "Flag Stop Station Leaves the Tracks." *Evening Bulletin*, February 3, 1975.

———. "Flag Stop Station Preserved." *Providence Journal Bulletin*, 1975.

———. "Smithfield Welfare Probe: It's Not the First." *Providence Evening Bulletin*, March 10, 1971.

Call. "Experts Call for Full Study, Survey of N.S. Historical Site." March 24, 2007, 1.

Cavanagh, Michael. "Native American Place Names of the Woonasquatucket River Valley." January 2004.

Chamberland, Normand H. "Woonsocket's Role Prominent in Chronology." *Woonsocket Call*, December 17, 1951.

Chapin, Howard M. "Illustrations of the Seals, Arms, and Flags of Rhode Island." Rhode Island, 1913.

———. "Seals as Coats-Of-Arms, Shields Bearing Appropriate Heraldic Designs Suggested for Rhode Island Towns." *Providence Sunday Journal*, September 16, 1928.

Davis, Thomas B. "District Schools of Smithfield, R.I. Before 1871." Unpublished research paper, Rhode Island, 1933.

Dexter, Vincent. "Greenville School Bell Fate Concerns All Says NP Historian." *Observer*, December 14, 1989.

———. "History in Ashes." (Woonsocket) *Independent*, December 9, 1984.

Eno, Paul F. "Across North County on a Trolley Car!" *Observer*, December 16, 1982.

Evening Bulletin. "Smithfield Council Endorses Permanent Police Force Bill Over Sullivan's Protest." Circa 2940s, 22.

———. "Two Lose Lives in Plane Crash in Smithfield." May 28, 1934.

Evening Call. "Arrest in Murder Case." January 8, 1908.

———. "Georgiaville Has a $50,000 Blaze." April 21, 1915.

———. "Head-On Collision." June 13, 1894, 4.

———. "Woman Murdered for $16." January 4, 1908, 1.

Hadden, Doug. "Firemen Commended in Stillwater Mill Blaze." *Observer*, July 19, 1984, 1.

———. "100 Years of History Lost in 100 Minutes." *Observer*, May 24, 1984.

Hazard, Thomas. "Report on the Poor and Insane in Rhode Island." Providence, 1851.

Historic Archeological Sites Inventory, Rhode Island Historical Preservation Commission, Smithfield Town Asylum Site, #RI 1870, June 1991. Rhode Island Historical Society collection.

Hurd, Beth. "Smithfield Police Canine Partnership Latest Tool to Deter Crime." *Your Smithfield* magazine, December 2008, 12.

Iannitelli, Ralph. "Klansmen Klonvocate at Georgiaville in '20's." *Observer*, August 7, 1969, 1.

Kennedy, Dennis. "An Old Statue Finds a New Home." *Observer*, October 24, 1991, 5A.

Lans, Kristen. "Bravery Fondly Recalled 25 Years after Tragedy." *Woonsocket Call*, May 21, 1994.

Marcus, Gina. "Old Smithfield Village Train Depot to Get a New Life." *Providence Journal Bulletin*, November 6, 1980.

Maroney, Agnes R. "Hanton City or Haunted City?" Paper presented to the Historical Society of Smithfield, 1936.

Mathews, Margery I. Letter to the Editor. *Observer*, June 15, 1972.

McVey, James H., deputy chief (ret.). "A Concise History" (of the Smithfield Police Department). November 19, 1990.

———. "A History of the Smithfield Police Department." Updated by Chief William A. McGarry, undated.

Morgan, Thomas J. "At Fidelity, Graveyard Shift Has Deep Historical Roots." *Providence Journal*, September 24, 2003, C.01.

———. "Gone But Not Forgotten." *Providence Journal*, December 11, 1998.

Mowry, Mary. "A Moving Station." *Observer*, December 6, 1979.

"The New Smithfield Police Station." Dedication Day Program, January 14, 1973.

New York Times. "Plane with Skydivers Crashes in Rhode Island." September 8, 1997.

Nipmuc History website, http://www.dickshovel.com/nipmuc.html.

Observer. "A Belated Gift from the Class of '31." January 10, 1985.

———. "Georgiaville Fire Company." February 8, 1962, 14.

———. "Greenville Fire Company." February 8, 1962, 13.

———. Letter to the Editor. May 10, 1962, 15.

———. "Mysterious Pillars Identified." June 1, 1972.

———. "Pond Patrol." September 4, 2003.

———. "Report of the Sfld. Planning Board to the Town Council Regarding the Establishment of a Wionkhiege Valley Fire District." May 10, 1962, 15.

———. "Smithfield 250 Anniversary." September 25, 1980, section B.

———. "The Story of Appleland." September 26, 1963.

———. "There Were Memories in the Firelight." May 11, 1961.

———. "Where Is the Water Witch?" October 1, 1970, 17.

———. "Wionkhiege Station." September 25, 1980, 23.

———. "Wionkhiege Valley Fire Co. Organized." September 18, 1958, 4.

———. "Wionkhiege Valley Volunteer Fire Company." February 8, 1962.

Pawtucket Times. "Pawtucket Lawyer Killed in R.I. Army Plane Crash." August 6, 1943, 1.

Plat of Enfield Mills sales booklet, May 1906.

Providence Journal. "Brown Senior Loses Life in Plane Crash." March 16, 1931, 1.

———. "A Buried City." October 6, 1889, 12.

———. "Fire Destroys Old Stillwater Mill." May 17, 1984.

———. Firefighter Raymond W. Segee Obituary. October 8, 1956, 11.

———. Letter to the Editor, October 24, 1870.

———. "The Lost Village." June 2, 1918, section 5, 7.

———. "One-Woman Golf Course at Stillwater—Developed on Appleby Ancestral Acres." February 3, 1933.

———. "Parents Watch in Horror." September 8, 1997.

———. "Smithfield's Legend of an Indian Tragedy." October 6, 1929.

———. "Three Men Perish in Bomber Crash." August 6, 1943, 1.

———. "Train Hits Auto, One Dead, 6 Hurt." September 19, 1945, 1.

———. "Two Men Killed in Plane Crash in Smithfield." November 18, 2008, B1.

Providence Journal Bulletin. "Boy, Policeman Drown in Reservoir." December 11, 1968, 1.

———. "Drowned Policeman Promoted." December 11, 1968, 26.

Providence Sunday Journal. "Need Repairs, Mr. Aviator? Drop in on Smithfield!" August 29, 1926.

———. "Permanent Police Force Is Opposed." Circa 1940s.

———. "Rhode Island's Lost Village Once Humming with Industry." October 2, 1927.

———. "Skeeterville and a Village Revived." January 22, 1905.

———. "Smithfield Woman Sells Her Golf Course." March 8, 1959, N42.

———. "Stones Left Unturned." April 15, 2007, 1.

"Report of the Committee of Investigation of Charges against the Overseer of the Poor, Commissioners of the Town Asylum, Keeper of the Town Asylum, and General Treatment of the Poor in the Town of Smithfield." Printed by Order of the Town of Smithfield: E.L. Freeman, 1870.

Sasso, Laurence J., Jr. "Retired Deputy Chief Is Author of Short History of the Force." *Your Smithfield* magazine, January 2008, 56.

———. "They Dropped in for Christmas." *Observer*, December 16, 1993, section B.

Scopelliti, Ron. "Police Dept. Working Toward Re-Accreditation." *Observer*, February 10, 2005.

———. "A Police Station on Wheels." *Observer*, January 27, 2005, 1.

Smithfield Police Department ordinance adopted May 28, 1937. Town Council book 9, 18.

Smithfield Police report of death of Officer Vezina, December 10, 1968.

State of Rhode Island, Division of Fire Safety. Report on the Stillwater Mill Fire, Complaint # 2-2040, 1984

Strickland, Franklin N. "Curious Smithfield Rock Made a Natural Threshing Floor for Pioneer Farmers and Perhaps Indians before Them." *Providence Journal*, February 14, 1937.

Sullivan, Joseph W. "Rhode Island's Invisible Empire: A Demographic Glimpse into the Ku Klux Klan." *Rhode Island History* 47, no. 2 (May 1989).

Sunday Call. "The Mystery of the Mounds." February 18, 2007, 1.

———. "New Mounds Discovery Raises Questions about Future of Historic Area." May 20, 2007, 1.

Tanner, Martha O. "Exploring the Rumbly—Threshing Rock Is Part of Hanton City." *Observer*, May 25, 1972.

———. "Hanton City Revisited." *Observer*, August 10, 1972.

Time magazine. "The Skip Does It." January 18, 1943.

Urenbeck, Lou. "Target: Origin of 'Lost Village.'" *Providence Journal*, 1973.

Whipple, Dorothy. "The Old Greenville Tavern." *Hinterlander*, Western Rhode Island Civil Historical Society, May 24, 1949.

Wood, W. Edward. "Crime Witnesses Lived in Guarded Smithfield House." *Providence Journal*, May 28, 1974.

Woonsocket Call. "Brown Student Dies As Plane Crashes Down." March 16, 1931.

———. "D&B Used 12 Miles of Wire for No. Central Airport Job!" December 17, 1951.

———. "Driver Killed as Auto Rams Slow Freight." September 29, 1955, 1.

———. "Guard of Honor on Duty at Bier—Wilkins Rites Tomorrow." May 29, 1934.

———. "High Winds Ground Planes for Dedication of Airport." December 17, 1951, 1.

———. "Impressive Rites Held for Victims of Plane Crash." May 31, 1934.

———. "Man, 3 Women Dead, Result of Crash At Smithfield Crossing." April 15, 1925, 1.

———. "North Central State Airport Dedication Set." December 14, 1951, 1.

———. "Two Men Killed as Plane Crashes Near Landing Field." May 28, 1934.

———. "Utilities Board to Probe Fatal Crash." April 15, 1925, 1.

———. "Woonsocket Flyer Escapes Serious Injury as Plane Crashes Near Smithfield Airport." August 26, 1940.

Woonsocket Patriot. "Another Railroad to Woonsocket." July 19, 1872, 1.
———. "The Branch Railway." February 21, 1873.
———. "Burrillville." April 19, 1872, 1.
———. "Georgiaville." December 11, 1884.
———. "Georgiaville—Homicide." November 8, 1872, 1.
———. "Georgiaville—Something New." December 25, 1874, 1.
———. "Greenville Branch Railroad." March 7, 1873.
———. "The Greenville Branch Railroad." May 22, 1874, 1.
———. "Greenville—Fire." June 24, 1870.
———. "Greenville Items." August 26, 1870.
———. "Greenville—Protection against Fire." July 29, 1870.
———. "Greenville—Railroad Matters." January 29, 1875, 1.
———. "Greenville—Railroad Meeting." November 24, 1871, 2.
———. "Greenville—The Branch Railroad." May 8, 1874, 1.
———. "Greenville—The Branch Railroad." November 28, 1872, 1.
———. "Is the Life of a Brakeman of Any Value?" August 16, 1872, 4.
———. "New Railroad to Providence." October 4, 1872, 1.
———. "Pascoag—New Railroad." August 22, 1873, 1.
———. "Proposed Railroad Extension." September 6, 1872, 1.
———. "Providence and Springfield Railroad." August 15, 1873, 1.
———. "Providence and Springfield Railroad." December 6, 1872, 1.
———. "Providence and Springfield Railroad." May 2, 1873.
———. Providence and Springfield Railroad advertisement. November 15, 1872, 6.
———. "Railroad Accident." December 27, 1878, 1.
———. "Rail Road Accident." June 27, 1835, 2.
———. "Railroad Accidents—Greenville." April 30, 1875, 1.
———. "Railroad Anniversary." October 27, 1876, 1.
———. "Railroad Matters." March 15, 1872, 1.
———. "Railroad to Greenville." January 24, 1873, 1.
———. "A Shocking Tragedy—A Woman Shot." September 5, 1873, 1.
———. "Smithfield." February 24, 1871, 2.
———. "Smithfield—Charges against Overseers of Town Asylum." December 2, 1870, 2.
———. "Smithfield—First Town Council Meeting." June 23, 1871.
———. "Smithfield—Railroad Crossings." February 4, 1876, 1.
———. "Smithfield—Re-Building of Stillwater Woolen Mill." August 23, 1872, 1.
———. "Smithfield—The Division of the Town." December 24, 1870.
———. "Smithfield—The Town Asylum." November 11, 1870, 2.

———. "Smithfield—The Town Asylum." October 28, 1870, 2.
———. "Smithfield—The Town to Be Divided into Three Towns." January 27, 1871.
———. "Smithfield—Town Council." June 30, 1871.
———. "Smithfield—Town Council." March 7, 1873, 1.
———. "Smithfield—Town Council." November 4, 1870, 2.
———. "Smithfield—Town Meeting." May 23, 1873.
———. "Smithfield—Town Meeting." October 13, 1871, 2.
———. "Stillwater—Destruction of the Woolen Mill." June 28, 1872, 1.
———. "What's in a Name?" March 31, 1871.
———. "Woonasquatucket Railroad." April 5, 1872, 1.
———. "Woonasquatucket Railroad." April 12, 1872, 1.
———. "Woonasquatucket Railroad." June 28, 1872, 1.
———. "Woonasquatucket Valley Railroad." February 18, 1870.
Your Smithfield magazine. "Wampanoag Chief Pleads Protection for Sacred Grounds." June 2007, 48.

Some of the aviation accident information was supplied by Lawrence Webster, aviation archaeologist and historian, Charlestown, Rhode Island.

About the Author

Jim has spent many hours exploring the woods of northern Rhode Island searching for lost historic sites, including abandoned colonial-era farms and those connected with possible Native American activity. He has located and documented many sites in Smithfield, some of which are mentioned in this book.

In 2003, he learned of a forgotten World War II military plane crash that occurred on Smithfield's Wolf Hill, in which three servicemen lost their lives. Due to wartime secrecy and the passage of time, there was some mystery surrounding the event. By obtaining a copy of the now declassified military investigation report, Jim was able to present for the first time the complete story of the incident, which can be found on Smithfield's town website at www.smithfieldri.com.

Jim's interest in history goes back to his youth, but it is only in recent years that he has begun to write about it. He is active with the Historical Society of Smithfield and belongs to the New England Antiquities Research Association. Jim is also the author of *Forgotten Tales of Rhode Island* (The History Press, 2008).